Finding the True Self

Finding the True Self

Talks of the Seon Mountain Monk
Jinje

Collected Teachings of Jinje Beopwon Sunim,
Head of the Korean Jogye Order

Lotus Lantern Books
One Magnificent Mile
980 N. Michigan Avenue, Suite 1400
Chicago, IL 60611
www.lotuslanternbooks.com

9 8 7 6 5 4 3 2 1

Printed in Republic of Korea

Finding the True Self: Talks of the Seon Mountain Monk Jinje: Collected Teachings of Jinje Beopwon Sunim, Head of the Korean Jogye Order / by Jinje.
ISBN 978-0-9961027-1-1 (pbk)

Lotus Lantern Books titles may be purchased for educational and promotional uses by special sales. For more information, please contact the publisher, Hyeryun Lee Park by e-mail to hleepark@lotuslanternbooks.com.

Author: Jinje; Editors: Koun Franz & Ven. Keumseong; Translation: Hong Hee Yeon, Jhin Wookee, & Heewon Park; Proofreading: Ven. Dowon; Book Design: SOYO; Artwork: Ven. Tongchic; Prodction Planning: Ko Joori; On-site Production: Yun Chan-Mok;

Distributed in United States and Canada by Lotus Lantern Books

Conventions

"Seon" (also seen transcribed as Sŏn) is the Korean pronunciation of the Chinese character for "Zen," the more familiar Japanese pronunciation of the same word. Although Seon and Zen (as well as Chinese "Chan" and Vietnamese "Thien") are simply different lingual pronunciations referring to the same school of Sinitic Buddhism, "Seon" is used here since this book deals specifically with the Korean tradition of this school.

"Sunim" (more correctly transcribed as Seunim or Sŭnim) is the Korean word for a monk or a nun, and refers to any ordained cleric in the Buddhist order, from the youngest novice to the eldest Seon master. This term is used throughout this book in referring to Buddhist monks and nuns in order to convey the distinctive flavor of the Korean Seon tradition.

"Sa" is a Koran word for a Buddhist temple (Vihara or Sangharama in Sanskrit):
For example, "Donghwa-sa" means "Donghwa Buddhist Temple."

Korean transcriptions generally follow the latest Republic of Korea national Romanization system.

TABLE OF CONTENTS

Foreword

It has been my pleasure to know Seon Master Jinje for more than thirty years. We first met at the mountain retreat of Ilta Sunim, who was renowned for his study of vinaya and his ascetic practices. Since then, Master Jinje has come to hold a unique place in Korean Buddhist life. He was trained in the traditional monastic style of meditation, which required retreat from ordinary life, but his subsequent efforts have been directed toward people living in the ever-growing urban areas of Korea.

The large complex he has developed at Haeunjeong-sa is located on a mountainside at the very edge of downtown Busan. Facing the main hall, one has a view of mountains and forests. When one turns in the other direction and looks out toward the sea, there spreads out below a vast complex of high-rise buildings. One feels that his monastery is like an island floating above the busy and vibrant life of the city. The location is an expression of his attempt to preserve the values of the quietude of the mountain for reflection and contemplation while at the same time to maintain easy access for millions of people in the city below it. This combination of mountain and city is hard to create and sustain. Master Jinje has accomplished it with skill and a deep feeling of compassion for the people who live their lives in the work and stress of a modern city. One is reminded of the ten oxherding episodes, where the final scene for the meditator is the ability to reenter the marketplace of human activity. In many ways the activities of his monastery reflect the need to have the enlightened ones among us. It also shows us a living example of how a contemporary Buddhist master can express this reentry to the "marketplace."

Jinje Sunim's teachings, as presented in this volume, are traditional and yet contemporary in application. Our mind is ever a focus for his attention because it is the mind that is the seat of experience. However, he reminds us that the search for our "mind" can never result in finding a fixed and

unchanging entity. Every moment is a new experience; this is true whether we are in a mountain monastery or standing in the midst of a vast city that roars around us.

The application of *hwadu*, a dialogue expressing the wisdom of a questioner and the possibility of awakening this same wisdom in a responder, is at the heart of his practice and instruction. It is the shock of the unexpected, the sharpness of the rejection of normal discourse that is needed to shatter the strong defenses and barriers so deeply embedded in our psyche. Master Jinje presses for the adoption of this particular approach of the Korean Seon tradition. He feels that it is essential to have the moment when sudden enlightenment floods the mind While meditation is often a path to this singular event, he wishes to remind us that no activity can ease one into enlightenment. A shift of such magnitude in the way our minds process experience requires a method that is radical and utterly transforming. Often we hear this described as "sudden" enlightenment, but it may perhaps best be described as "whole" or "entire." This means that there is nothing omitted from the transformation of view of that moment.

In this volume, Master Jinje shares his thoughts and insights about this method with the goal of bringing awareness of hwadu practice to people everywhere. His message is shared in poetic formulations that are as pleasing to read as they are instructive.

Lewis Lancaster
Chen Professor Emeritus of Buddhist Studies
Department of East Asian Languages and Cultures
University of California, Berkeley

Opening Verse

**"Heaven and Earth share the same root with me;
All things in the universe and I together comprise one body."
Hearing this, an ancient man says, "A sage with the perfected
Wisdom eye reckons such words as those in a dream."
With his wisdom eye of truth, he will be a teacher in the realms of
Gods and humans.**

Once one sees the true nature and attains the wisdom eye of truth, it is
eternal. Everyone has a secret storehouse with an inexhaustible bounty
of treasures—how can it ever be depleted? The life of a sage who has
finished his work is immutable for a thousand lives and ten thousand
kalpas to come. In the moment that one knows and attains this, the path is
suddenly realized.

Darkness is originally in light, so do not say that one meets another
because of darkness. Light is in darkness, so do not say that one sees
another by way of light. Where all Dharmas cease to exist, they certainly
exist in eternity; when all Dharmas arise, they are in utter emptiness and
eternal stillness. The path is suddenly realized.

Life is in death, and death is in life.

Everyone in the Four Seas and Five Lakes[1]! If you wish to know the world of truth, sincerely look for your true self in everyday life, whether awake or asleep.

To cast a fishing line is to reel in the horse and
The dragon of stellar constitution.
All subtle and profound words beyond form or convention
Are to find the one with clear eyes who sees this mountain monk.

Jinje Beopwon
Supreme Patriarch, Jogye Order of Korean Buddhism
Republic of Korea

---

1 The whole world.

RAISING THE DHARMA STAFF:
SEON TALKS

The talks that follow are intended to convey the Dharma with more than just words. Each is a highly ritualized expression in itself with critical moments that cannot be seen on the page. As readers, we are invited to visualize this encounter.

Before a talk begins, Master Jinje is seated before the assembly and chants the Three Refuges and the Heart Sutra with the members of the fourfold community (monks, nuns, laymen, and laywomen). When the chanting is finished, two ordained representatives come forward to offer three prostrations as a request for the teaching. Accepting the request, the master rises and takes his place on the Dharma seat, at which point the entire assembly makes three more prostrations in request.

Three claps of a bamboo stick signal the commencement of meditation, which lasts up to five minutes. Three more claps mark the end.

Seated before the assembly in the meditation posture, the master is utilizing the physical body to open the gates of understanding; the teaching is already complete. But few can understand such a direct teaching. So with his right hand he lifts up the Dharma staff, holding it horizontally for all to see. In this powerful gesture, he illuminates the world of truth. This electric moment is the true start of each talk.

Even though nothing is lacking in this presentation of the Dharma, the master knows not everyone understands the full meaning of what has been expressed; he looks out over the faces of those gathered, cradles the staff against his left shoulder, and begins to speak. He opens with a verse, the very heart of the teaching. The talk moves from there into the path of training, then often to anecdotes and teachings from previous Dharma masters. Master Jinje concludes with a turning phrase of his own and strikes the staff on the ground one last time, punctuating the talk's end and dedicating the day's merit to all sentient beings.

What Is the Sound of the Buddha's Voice?

November 6, 1991, at Haeunjeong-sa

What is the sound of the Buddha's voice when he teaches the Dharma?

The Diamond Sutra says:
Whoever sees me by my likeness,
Whoever seeks me in the sound of my voice —
Depraved are his footsteps upon the path,
For he cannot perceive the true Buddha.

Do you understand?

How can we see the true Buddha unconstrained by sound and sight? The more we try to see, the farther away is the Buddha—tens of thousands of miles away. Lady Maya, Shakyamuni Buddha's mother, passed away one week after he was born. For giving birth to the greatest saint the world has ever seen, she was rewarded with a rebirth in Indra's Heaven, where thirty-three gods reside.

After Shakyamuni Buddha attained full enlightenment, he elucidated the buddhaDharma to sentient beings in the mundane world. He was then invited to Indra's heaven and gave Dharma teachings there for ninety days to repay the debt to his mother for her previous gift of life.

While Shakyamuni Buddha was away in Indra's heaven, a powerful Indian king, missing the Buddha desperately, summoned skilled craftsmen and ordered them to sculpt a statue in his image. Master artisans gathered from all over the country and painstakingly reproduced his likeness in sandalwood, perfect in every respect.

All thirty-two primary marks and eighty secondary marks present on the body of a Buddha were meticulously and faithfully depicted. Only one thing was missing; the voice of the Buddha teaching the Dharma. The mark of sound was missing.

What, then, is the auditory mark of excellence, the manifestation of the sound of the Buddha's voice when he teaches the Dharma?

I am afraid that someone nearby may hear.

When Shakyamuni Buddha finally finished his visit to Indra's heaven and came back to the human realm, all the 1200 disciples of his sangha thronged to greet him.

There was a bhiksuni named Uppalavanna in the crowd. Her complexion was as fair as a blue lotus, and she was considered the foremost in supernormal powers. She thought, "I am a bhiksuni, so my turn to greet the Buddha will come only after principle disciples and bhiksus. I am going to use my supernatural power to be the first to see him!" She transformed herself into a *cakravarti-raja* (wheel-turning sage king), came toward the front of the assembly, and bowed to the Buddha.

However, the Buddha scolded her severely: "You may have skirted the sangha's rule and managed to be the first person to greet me," he said, "but you saw only my physical body and failed to see my Dharma body. Subhuti on the other hand, while sitting peacefully under a rock in the mountains, has witnessed my Dharma body without moving a single step."

People in the secular world believe someone is enlightened only when he or she displays supernatural powers, calling them marvelous and mysterious. However, those are merely tricks, barely worth a few coins. If you try to attain Dharma by seeking appearances, you will never find the true Dharma. The true Dharma can be known only when your eyes are open and no longer limited by the confines of form.

One day, the Buddha came back from collecting alms from seven households, finished his meal, washed his feet, and sat in silent meditation.

Suddenly, his disciple Subhuti stood up, put his palms together, and bowed. Then he praised the Buddha, "Oh, World-Honored One! It is truly marvelous and mysterious!"

Do you understand? How did Subhuti meet with the Buddha while sitting under a rock far away? Furthermore, what wondrous truth did Subhuti see that made him exclaim "marvelous and mysterious" when the Buddha was sitting in silence, not uttering a single word?

The body of a villain that steals and cheats has been revealed.

There Are No Saints

April 17, 2011, at Donghwa-sa

Where does the wisdom lie in Bodhidharma's nine years of facing the wall?

To snag and stop a black stallion that runs 1,000 miles,
Throw a lasso that extends 10,000 miles.
To harvest a gigantic whale that spurts jets of gushing water,
Cast a net that blanks the whole sky.

Master Bodhidharma was born a prince of the Pallava Dynasty in southern India. He renounced this world and became a disciple of Prajnatara. He attained enlightenment and was eventually elevated to the exalted position of the 28th Patriarch of Buddhism in an uninterrupted line of direct succession that extends all the way back to the Buddha himself.

Master Bodhidharma realized that there was no one in India to whom he could transmit his Dharma. But his wisdom eye revealed that the causes and conditions in China were ripe to embrace the supreme teaching of the Buddha and cultivate great teachers to pass on the buddhaDharma. When Bodhidharma reached Guangzhou, China, after an arduous journey from India, Emperor Wu of the Liang Dynasty heard of him and invited him to the imperial court.

Emperor Wu was a fervent patron of Buddhism. During his reign, the country became dotted with splendid monasteries and pagodas, and monastic communities received abundant financial support. The emperor's faith and devotion was such that when he donned a monastic robe and gave a teaching on Buddhism, light radiated from him and flowers rained down from the sky, earning him the nickname the "Bodhisattva Emperor."

The Emperor asked Bodhidharma: "How much merit have I accrued for building monasteries and pagodas and having sutras copied all my life?" Bodhidharma answered, "None whatsoever."

Accumulating good karma by virtuous deeds is different from gaining merit through correct spiritual practice. Constructing monasteries, erecting pagodas, and sponsoring monks indeed bring good karma but do not necessarily earn merit. Ignorant of this, Emperor Wu was confused when told that all his generosity would gain him no merit at all.

The emperor asked him again. "So, what is the highest truth of the saints' Dharma?" The master replied, "It is wide open and bare — there are no saints."

The truth is limitlessly vast like empty space; no discrimination can take root, not even the designation of a saint. If enlightened saints do not exist, how can ordinary sentient beings exist?

Emperor Wu asked yet again. "Who, then, is standing and speaking before me?" The master said, "I know not."

Though zealously devout and pious, this so-called "Bodhisattva Emperor" woefully lacked the wisdom eye that recognizes truth. The ordinary mind that asks conventional questions cannot cope with the answers produced by an enlightened mind. Once it became obvious that he had failed to communicate and connect with the emperor, Master Bodhidharma left the palace immediately, crossed the Yangtze River and traveled to the Wei Dynasty in northern China, where he then spent nine years in meditation staring at the wall of his cave.

Still puzzled, Emperor Wu summoned Master Baozhi Zhigong, one of the most esteemed Buddhist teachers of the time. The emperor asked him about the encounter with Master Bodhidharma. Master Baozhi then asked the Emperor, "Does Your Majesty still not know who he is?"

"No, I do not."

"He is a manifestation of Avalokiteshvara, who deigns to come to China to transmit the Dharma of Buddha's heart seal."

The emperor regretted letting Master Bodhidharma leave. He was about to dispatch a messenger to go and beg Bodhidharma to return, but Master Baozhi stopped him, saying, "Your Majesty, do not send a messenger to fetch him. Even if every subject of the Liang Kingdom begged on their knees for the master's return, he still would not come back."

Meanwhile, Bodhidharma had arrived at the Shaolin Monastery in the northern kingdom of Wei and secluded himself in a cave nearby. Because he had meditated gazing at a wall for nine years, not speaking for the entire time, people started calling him "a wall-gazing Brahman."

Do you understand the true meaning of the words spoken to Emperor Wu by Bodhidharma?

If you fathom the essence of this truth, Master Bodhidharma will be so delighted that he will grace this assembly with his presence. Can you see what Bodhidharma meant by, "It is wide open and bare — there is no saint"?

Even a thousand saints cannot walk the path together.

Now tell me, do you grasp the true meaning of why Master Bodhidharma gave the cryptic answer, "I know not, Your Majesty" to Emperor Wu's question, "Who is standing and speaking before me?"

It is like blundering on toward a mishap through indiscretion.

So where does the wisdom lie in Bodhidharma's nine years of facing the wall?

An old man with blocky front teeth grew a three-foot long beard.

Master Bodhidharma spent nine years in silent practice, only gazing at the wall of his cave dwelling, before fate brought him a disciple worthy of receiving his Dharma seal. It was a monk named Shenguang who had scoured the vast expanse of China looking for an enlightened master to teach him the ultimate truth of the Buddha's great path. He searched in vain until someone pointed him toward Bodhidharma's cave.

When Shenguang finally arrived at the cave, however, Bodhidharma refused to turn away from the wall or even acknowledge his presence. Nevertheless, Shenguang prostrated himself on the ground and pleaded with the master, saying, "I came to attain the truth of the Buddha's great path." But the master continued to ignore him.

When the encounter between Shenguang and Master Bodhidharma took place, it was bitterly cold and a howling blizzard swept the landscape. Shenguang kept a vigil in front of the master's cave as the freezing wind battered him. The blizzard raged all night, burying him in snow to the waist. Imagine how cold it must have been! However, Shenguang dismissed all bodily discomfort and pain in his desperate resolve to attain the great Dharma.

A full day and night passed before Master Bodhidharma gave a curt glance toward Shenguang. Finding him still standing motionless, waist deep in snow with his palms together, the master finally turned around, looked Shenguang squarely in the face, and abruptly asked him, "Why did you come here?"

"I came to learn the true Dharma of the Buddha."

"You want to learn Buddha's true Dharma? His supreme teaching can be experienced and attained only if, after uncountable eons of the most diligent practice, you can effortlessly do that which is undoable, and after you can leisurely conquer the pain that is unconquerable. How dare the likes of you with your shoddy faith and scant devotion aspire to attain the true Dharma?"

Even the fervor that had driven Shenguang to brave the piercing cold and waist deep snow for a full day seemed hardly adequate.

As soon as Master Bodhidharma's speech ended, Shenguang drew a knife that he carried at his side and cut off his left arm. He was demonstrating his fierce aspiration to attain the supreme Dharma, in total disregard for his body, even for his life.

Master Bodhidharma must have thought that was sufficient, because he granted Shenguang a permission: "If there is a question that troubles your mind, ask." Shenguang said to Bodhidharma, "My mind is anxious. Please pacify it."

All sentient beings are born with an anxious mind. This is indeed the karma of ordinary beings.

Bodhidharma replied, "Bring me your mind, and I will pacify it."

Taken by surprise, Shenguang frantically searched for it, but to no avail. Finally, he admitted, "Although I've sought it, I cannot find it."

"There," Bodhidharma shouted, "I have pacified your mind."

At this, Shenguang's mind opened.

As they were connected in the realm of truth, Master Bodhidharma accepted Shenguang as his disciple and bestowed on him a new Dharma name, Dazu Huike.

When Master Bodhidharma realized that his time on earth was drawing to an end, he called together all his disciples and asked, "The causes and conditions that have kept me in this land are dissipating. Can each of you say something to demonstrate your understanding?"

A monk named Daofu stepped forward and said, "It is not bound by words and phrases, nor is it separate from words and phrases. This is the function of the path."

The master said, "You have attained my skin."

The nun Zongchi stepped up and said, "It is like a glorious glimpse taken by Ananda of the realm of Akshobhya Buddha. Seen once, it need not be seen again."

The master replied, "You have attained my flesh."

The monk Daoyu stood up and declared, "The four elements of the body are all empty. The five skandhas are without actual existence. Not a single Dharma can be grasped by human intention or emotion."

Master Bodhidharma answered, "You have attained my bones."

Finally, Huike came forth, bowed deeply three times in silence and stood up straight.

Master Bodhidharma said, "You have attained my marrow." He then passed on the monastic robe and alms bowl of Dharma succession to Huike, making him the Second Patriarch of the Chinese Chan tradition after himself—a guardian entrusted to keeping the lantern of truth burning brightly.

Bodhidharma broke down and laid bare the progress of each student on the path of truth for all to see. Now, can you fathom the unfathomable depth of Master Bodhidharma's Dharma?

Attaining skin, flesh, bone, and marrow!
A blue-eyed old man from the southern region
Is not allowed the knowing of truth.
A blue-eyed old man from the southern region
Is allowed the knowing of truth.

The schools of Buddhism that thrived in China during Master Bodhidharma's time focused mostly on scripture-based doctrinal studies. However, Master Bodhidharma taught that "any practice based on forms perceivable by unenlightened beings, including all scriptures, can never fully address and resolve the matter of life and death. One can attain Buddhahood only by pointing directly at one's mind and seeing its true nature." This statement challenged the very foundation of the prestige these schools had enjoyed up until then. Feeling threatened, they tried to assassinate Bodhidharma on multiple occasions, including six attempts to poison him. The poison they used against him was so devastatingly deadly that when the master spat out the poisoned food on a rock, it cracked.

Every time he was served poisoned food, Master Bodhidharma sensed it. But on the sixth attempt on his life, knowing his time had come, he just swallowed the poison—even though fully aware of it—and entered parinirvana. Such an act would be unimaginable for an ordinary being. Only those who wield sublime capabilities borne out of the most rarified stage of attainment on the path can commit such a magnificent act.

Master Bodhidharma's body was placed in a stone sarcophagus and interred in a tomb on Mount Xionger. However, three years after his burial, Ambassador Song Yun of northern Wei, on his way back from his mission to the western regions, saw him walking and holding a shoe at Pamir Heights.

"Master, where are you going?"

"I am going home to India."

"This is too soon! We still need you in China to propagate far and wide the noble and lofty teaching of the Buddha."

"The causes and conditions that brought me to China are no more."

The ambassador bade him farewell and continued his journey to northern Wei. When he arrived at the palace, he told the emperor about his encounter.

"What an outrageous lie!" replied the emperor. "He was interred with great ceremony on Mount Xionger three years ago."

But Song Yun would not budge. "No, I really saw him in the mountains of Pamir and exchanged words with him!" The emperor was finally persuaded of the truth of Song Yun's account and had the grave exhumed. When the sarcophagus was opened, it contained only a single shoe.

We can all be as completely free of hindrances as Master Bodhidharma when we reach such an unsurpassedly exalted stage. First, through Seon practice, shed a clear light on the seal of wisdom innate in all of our hearts. Then, the marvelous capabilities demonstrated by Master Bodhidharma will naturally unfold and permeate us over time. We can all become wholly liberated beings with carefree dignity, exactly like Master Bodhidharma himself. But if you have accomplished very little, despite a lifetime of meditation practice, it is because you fail to surrender yourself entirely to the seeking of this one thought focused on your hwadu. Then, sitting meditation is merely a waste of time—time spent lost in a quagmire of wretched delusions.

If you investigate a hwadu with a fervent determination to resolve this matter of life and death in this very life, at any cost, you will not notice the passage of time. You will not notice people making a racket around you. You will even forget you are sitting in meditation. Only one thought will remain, singularly focused on the hwadu. When this hwadu single-mindedness begins to flow unceasingly, your eyes will open to the truth. This is true for everyone, without exception.

Where do you think Master Bodhidharma abides now, after having lived such a spectacular life of Dharma?

Look, look again! Here comes Bodhidharma!

No Place for Dust

May 12, 2009, at Haeunjeong-sa

Once you see your true nature,
all the karma of countless generations perishes without a trace.

Expound the most supreme and profound Dharma,
Causing all past, present, and future buddhas to turn tail and hide
three thousand miles away,
And ensnaring all past, present, and future patriarchs in an iron
cage.

How can one shake it off and survive?

Heaving a despondent sigh, "Alas!"
Moaning the dead and wailing, "Heavens!"

Sublime truth permeates the sighing of "Alas!" and the wailing of "Heavens!"
Only the perfect understanding of such profound Dharma will grant us the unhindered capability to wield upward truth and downward truth and exalt the Dharma to all sentient beings.

The Fifth Patriarch Hongren, direct Dharma descendent of Master Bodhidharma, established a sangha and taught the mind of the Buddha directly to hundreds of monks, but he was unable to find a true disciple to whom his enlightened mind could be directly transmitted. At that time, there was a young man with the last name Lu who had lost his father early and supported his widowed mother by cutting and selling firewood. One day, Lu went to the market, and upon hearing a monk reciting the Diamond Sutra, his mind opened wide and became awakened. Lu asked the monk, "Your chanting fills me with such a divine joy and makes me want to renounce this world. Which monastery are you from?" The monk said, "The Fifth Patriarch Hongren leads an assembly of several hundred monks on Mt. Huangmei. That's where you should go."

Greatly inspired, Lu bade farewell to his mother and immediately set off on foot to Mt. Huangmei. When Lu presented himself to the assembly, the Fifth Patriarch asked him, "Who are you and what do you seek?"

Lu replied, "Your disciple is a commoner from Lingnan. I have travelled thousands of miles to pay homage to you and seek nothing other than Buddhahood."

"So you're a barbarian from Lingnan! How can you expect to become a buddha?" asked the Patriarch.

Lu answered, "Although people are described as northerners and southerners, there is no distinction of north or south in buddhanature. A barbarian may differ from your eminence in body, but what difference exists in buddhanature?"

The Fifth Patriarch took note of Lu's brilliance, but he did not openly acknowledge it lest those listening become jealous. So the Patriarch dismissed Lu, assigning him lowly chores at the monastery's rice mill. There, Lu pounded rice and chopped wood for the next eight months.

One day, the Fifth Patriarch summoned the entire assembly and announced, "Write down what you've learned and what you've attained so far and bring it to me. If I find anyone who has attained the correct wisdom eye, I will bestow on him my monastic robe and alms bowl, designating him my Dharma successor and the Sixth Patriarch."

Shenxiu was a senior monk in the Fifth Patriarch's sangha who lectured and disciplined hundreds of junior monks. He spent days calculating, comparing, and conceptualizing his reply. Then one night, he snuck out in the wee hours past midnight and inscribed a verse on the wall of the southern corridor:

The body is the bodhi tree;
The mind is like a bright mirror's stand.
At all times polish it diligently,
Letting no dust or stain alight.

The next morning, Master Hongren saw this verse and declared, "Those who continue to cultivate mind diligently relying on this gatha will be spared rebirth in the the realms of hell, hungry ghosts, and animals." A few days later, Lu heard a novice monk passing by the rice mill reciting Shenxiu's gatha and asked him, "Can you tell me what verse you are reciting?"

"I am memorizing this verse because the master said we can avoid rebirth in the lower three realms of samsara if we practice it repeatedly."

Lu asked the novice monk, "I have composed a verse too. Would you write it down on the wall for me?" and recited it to him.

Bodhi is fundamentally without any tree;
The bright mirror is also not a stand.
Fundamentally, there is not a single thing,
Where could any dust alight?

The next morning, Master Hongren saw this verse as he passed the wall and found it exceptional. But, afraid his praise would incite the jealousy of the other monks, he denounced it, saying, "This author has not seen the true nature of mind yet," and had the verse scraped off.

However, the master secretly came to the rice mill later, sought out Lu and asked him, "Have you finished pounding the rice?"

Lu replied: "The pounding has been long done, but the rice has not been sifted from the chaff yet," implying that he had not yet received the transmission of Dharma. The Patriarch tapped the mill three times with his staff and returned to his room, indicating for Lu to enter his room at the third watch of the night.

Lu understood the master's signal and went to see him at the designated hour. Master Hongren was waiting for Lu, and, after receiving him, covered the door of his room with his robe to keep the light from escaping. The Fifth Patriarch was taking every precaution because meeting a true disciple required extraordinarily auspicious circumstances. He received Lu and expounded on the Diamond Sutra to him. When he came to the passage, "Generate and use mind without abiding," Lu's mind was completely penetrated and he attained a great awakening. He expressed it by composing this verse:

> How else would I have known that
> The self-nature is originally pure;
> The self-nature neither arises nor ceases to exist;
> In the nature of self, all Dharmas are perfectly consummated;
> The self-nature neither moves nor is at rest; and
> All myriad Dharmas are generated from this self-nature!

Upon hearing this, Master Hongren passed him his robe and bowl as a symbol of his approval and conferred the Dharma name Huineng on his new Dharma heir. He then sent him off into the night with the mandate, "Proclaim Dharma to the world when the time is ripe. Wait in hiding until then."

The next day, pandemonium broke out when the assembly discovered that a lowborn apprentice had received the Dharma seal of the Fifth Patriarch. Enraged monks organized a search party and pursued him, but Master Huineng evaded them. Fifteen years passed, and then one day, Master Huineng arrived at Faxingsi Monastery in Guangzhou, where Master Yinzong was giving a lecture on the Nirvana Sutra. Upon Master Huineng's arrival, the wind blew and a banner fluttered. Seeing this, two monks started arguing furiously over whether it was the wind that moved or the banner that moved. Master Huineng went forward and announced to the stunned assembly, "It is neither the wind nor the banner that moves. It is your mind that is moving."

Master Yinzong said, "Long ago I heard that the robe and bowl of Mt. Huangmei had come south. Might you be the one who received them?" When Master Huineng showed him the robe and bowl, Master Yinzong prostrated himself and had Preceptor Zhigyang initiate the ceremony for Master Huineng to take the monastic precepts, finally making him a fully ordained monk. Master Huineng was 39 years old.

Afterwards, the Sixth Patriarch presided at Baolinsi Monastery on Mt.

Caoxi and instructed the monks who flocked to Mt. Caoxi from far and wide, forming a flourishing sangha. One day, Qingyuan Xingsi sought an audience with the Patriarch and asked, "What should I do so as not to backslide and fall down into the practice done in stages?"

The Sixth Patriarch answered the question with another question. "What have you practiced and cultivated so far?"

Xingsi answered, "I have not practiced anything, not even the Dharma of all saints and sages."

The master asked again, "Then what stage of practice have you fallen into?"

Xingsi said, "What stages can there be when no Dharma of saints and sages has ever been practiced?"

Regarding their dialogue, one could say, "The head and the tail were interlaced beautifully," meaning their questions and answers flowed together seamlessly. This is how easy it is when the wisdom eye is open. The master was profoundly impressed by Xingsi, and made him chief among his followers.

One day, the Sixth Patriarch asked the assembly during a Dharma talk, "I have a thing that shores up the heavens above and sustains the earth down below. It is brighter than the sun and the moon combined, and darker than the blackest lacquer. It has neither name nor form. It can neither be gathered nor grasped, yet it is invariably and eternally at work in everyday life, whether coming or going, walking or talking. Do you know what it is?"

Shenhui came forth and said, "It is the ultimate origin of all buddhas, and it is Shenhui's buddhanature."

The master said, "I just told you it has neither name nor form, yet you dare to recklessly apply names such as 'the ultimate origin of all buddhas' or 'Shenhui's buddhanature.' Even if you gain fame in the world later, you will become a monk of discursive knowledge and unenlightened understanding."

Sometime later, Nanyue Huairang penetrated all difficulties after fierce practice in an old hermitage. He came to Mt. Caoxi to meet the Sixth Patriarch. As the Sixth Patriarch sat and watched Huairang enter the room, he found Huairang's carriage noble and dignified, so he threw Huairang a question without preamble: "How would a thing come, whatever it is?"

Huairang replied, "The moment you define a single thing, it is already incorrect."

The Patriarch asked again, "Can it be cultivated and attained?"

Huairang said, "Attainment through cultivation may exist, but it is free from degradation or defilement."

Once you see your true nature, you leap onto the ground of the Tathagata, and all the karma of countless generations perishes without a trace. All of the karma of each and every sentient being in the ten directions, as numerous as the particles of dust on this great earth, is all restored and redeemed by the great wisdom of the Buddha; not even a shadow of affliction remains, nor any stain of defilement.

The Sixth Patriarch imparted a great teaching when he said, "This thing that cannot be tainted or defiled is protected by the mindfulness of all buddhas. You are already such as this; I am already such as this. Cherish and preserve this well. The 27th Patriarch, Prajnatara from western India, predicted 280 years ago that a pony would come under my tutelage and trample the people of the whole world to death. Do not go recklessly spreading Dharma." After hearing this, Huairang served as the Sixth Patriarch's attendant for fifteen years.

The tenet of "sudden enlightenment, sudden cultivation" is the only correct path to teaching one to see his or her true nature. The Sixth Patriarch, as well as the Fifth, was absolutely adamant about this. Shenxiu and Heze, each a disciple of the Sixth and Fifth Patriarchs, advocated the "gradual approach," and their view was inherited by Guifeng two hundred years later. There also have been teachers in Korea who were proponents of the gradual approach, until recently. However, you must understand that no eminent master or Patriarch of a true Seon lineage, looking all the way back to the Buddha himself, has ever championed the gradual approach. The Chan lineage of China branched into the Five Schools of Chan after Master Mazu Daoyi, but all of them exalted and relied on "sudden enlightenment, sudden practice" to guide their followers down the path toward true nature.

Lay a firm foundation of right teaching and right view. Only then can one see one's true nature and awaken to truth in this lifetime. You may tell yourself, "Oh, I will do it in my next life if I fail in this life, or my life after that." If your approach to the path of seeing your true nature is so frivolous and shallow as that, you will never achieve true awakening.

The Sixth Patriarch trained two towering giants of the flourishing Chan tradition, Qingyuan Xingsi and Nanyue Huairang, considered to be his two foremost disciples. Shitou Xiqian, Daowu Yuanzhi, Longtan, and Deshan Xuanjian traced their lineages back to Master Qingyuan, while Master Nanyue had six major disciples, among them Mazu Daoyi, Baizhang Huaihai, Huangbo Xiyun, and Linji Yixuan.

When the Sixth Patriarch saw that his time to enter parinirvana was near, he gathered all his followers and recited a verse:

> The mind-ground stores all the seeds of aspiration,
> Which all sprout and blossom in the rain that falls far and wide.
> Suddenly enlightened to the essence of a flower,
> The fruit of bodhi forms of itself.

The congregation asked him, "How soon will you return after you leave for Xinzhou[2]?"

The master said, "Leaves fall and revert to roots. Should I return, there would be no words." They asked further, "To whom has the correct Dharma been transmitted?" He replied, "Those who are enlightened have attained it; those in the state of no-mind have penetrated it."

After that, the Sixth Patriarch donned his formal monastic robe, sat upright, and entered parinirvana, calm and composed. The room filled with a mysterious fragrance, and a white rainbow shot up from the earth. His physical body was interred at Nanquan Monastery, and his relics are still revered today as having come from a living bodhisattva.

What do you think of the singular phrase of the cardinal truth?

A thousand speeches and ten thousand lectures of profound truth
Leave no impression on people's minds.
The sentences to follow are too long; I will deliver them tomorrow.

---

2 The Sixth Patriarch's hometown.

Teaching Upward, Teaching Downward

April 28, 1987, at Haeunjeong-sa

Essence and function are one.

Now perfectly unhindered in giving away and taking back,
Worry where all worries are exhausted.
Oh so pitiful are those who are stuck by words and
Snared by phrases!
Hair turned white while debating right and wrong.
Let go of all dichotomies and
Saunter languidly in the boundless meadow.

Huineng, the Sixth Patriarch of Chinese Chan Buddhism, was a bodhisattva in the flesh and the greatest saint among all the enlightened masters. The Sixth Patriarch trained many monks who became towering giants of the flourishing Chan tradition, and Qingyuan Xingsi and Nanyue Huairang were considered his two foremost disciples, both gifted in directly addressing people's needs and abilities and commanding their total attention. All five traditionally recognized houses of Chan were developed from the lineages of these two eminent masters.

The Caodong, Fayan, and Yunmen schools evolved from the teachings of Master Qingyuan, while Master Nanyue is the ancestor of the Linji and Guiyang Schools.

Shitou Xiqian, Daowu Yuanzhi, Longtan, and Deshan Xuanjian traced their lineage back to Master Qingyuan, while Master Nanyue had six major disciples including Mazu Daoyi, Baizhang Huaihai, Huangbo Xiyun, and Linji Yixuan. Therefore, it can be said that "Linji's roar" and "Deshan's blow" are related by birth, as both masters were direct Dharma descendents of the Sixth Patriarch.

The Seon tradition that earned the highest distinction in Korea—and is still paramount today—was passed down without interruption from these two true disciples of the Sixth Patriarch, with a closer kinship to Master Linji.

Twenty years ago, Seon Master Hyanggok asked this mountain monk the following question: "Which is more precious to you? Is it Deshan's way of teaching by dispensing beatings or Linji's way of shouting thunderously?"

So, this mountain monk answered, "Both masters deserve to be whacked thirty times by this Dharma staff."

Do you now understand these two great traditions of Seon that originated with the Sixth Patriarch himself?

If we are to revisit their teachings, Seon Master Qingyuan directed our spiritual endeavors upward to the essential nature of truth, while Seon Master Nanyue looked downward, showing us the function of truth, how to make unhindered use of it.

But in truth, essence and function are inseparable because they always form a united whole. Sometimes essence manifests itself as function, while function transforms itself into essence. Essence and function are one.

In unsurpassed perfect wisdom, if one knows the upward truth, he knows the downward truth as well; attaining the downward truth will naturally lead to the upward truth. Therefore, in reality, they are never divided; they are only referred to by two names.

Through Master Qingyuan and Master Nanyue, the two eminent luminaries of the early Chan lineage, the lofty and noble Dharma of the Sixth Patriarch spread doubly far and doubly wide.

One day, Master Qingyuan saw that the causes and conditions were perfect to confer the seal of Dharma transmission on one of his students and make him the head of another assembly. So the master summoned Shitou and entrusted him with a letter to Master Nanyue, saying, "If you deliver this letter to Master Nanyue and come back, I will present you with a dull axe. After that, you will reside on another mountain and lead your own sangha."

Shitou traveled several months on foot to reach Master Nanyue's monastery. As soon as he bowed to the master, Shitou boldly asked a challenging question, without even bothering to deliver the letter entrusted to him by his teacher. "How is it that one offers no adoration to the saints of all ages, nor respect to one's own spirituality?"

Facing such a lofty question, Master Nanyue asked back, "Why is it that your question points to only upward truth, and does not concern downward affairs?"

But Shitou pressed his point of view, saying, "Even if I am to be drowning in a sea of cyclical life and death for eons to come, I will still refuse to seek any teaching on nirvana presented either by buddhas or enlightened saints." Hearing this, Master Nanyue turned away from Shitou and said not another word.

The master found Shitou not worth so much as a look, for Shitou upheld only one side and disregarded the other, failing to see the whole.

Do you understand? If this mountain monk had been Master Nanyue, I would have scolded Shitou by saying, "You rascal! Enjoy roaming this boundless world blinded by the huge wooden plank you are carrying on your back." If so, his practice would have been greatly transformed.

Shitou retreated and went back to Master Qingyuan, who inquired, "Did you deliver the letter?"

"Neither the letter nor the faith has been commuted."

After relaying what happened with Master Nanyue in detail, Shitou pressed his case to Master Qingyuan.

"You said that you would give me a dull axe and allow me to reside on another mountain. Now, give me the axe."

Master Qingyuan simply lifted his foot in reply without saying a word. At this, Shitou's mind attained a great awakening. He prostrated himself before the master and received the transmission of Dharma. The master then installed Shitou with an assembly in another mountain.

The ancient sages took exquisitely meticulous heed of their students and entrusted them with the seal of Dharma only when their minds were perfectly persuaded. The process of Dharma transmission entailed such painstakingly scrupulous examination, for if it is not congruent with the path, even by just a pinprick, false Dharma will be a scourge that blinds sentient beings' eyes and eclipses the wisdom eye of the buddhas and patriarchs.

Why did the master lift his foot when asked for the dull ax, and why did Shitou bow?

In all eternal eons during which Dharma has been taught, it was seldom more difficult to understand than this question, for the infinite array of teachings are contained in this single exchange.

Do you understand?

If you fully realize the essence of upward truth,
How could you not be consummate in downward affairs!
Oh, downward!

Striking the Dharma staff on the ground.

This is it.

Taking the Student by the Nose

End of the 2012 winter retreat at Donghwa-sa

To attain the boundless world of truth on one's own is difficult.

When a prince is born, he is naturally honored on his own merits;
His deserved home is within the golden gates.
Worldly affairs already do not concern him upon birth.
He is in the jeweled palace with only his father, the king.

Every sentient being's most deeply rooted karma is the result of the three poisons: greed, hatred, and ignorance. Unless these are relinquished, one will never find peace. What must one do to be rid of these three unwholesome habits, gain supreme wisdom and perfect virtue, and attain the ultimate, unexcelled, perfect enlightenment of Buddhahood?

Today marks the last day of the winter retreat. Practitioners must ask themselves, "Have I wasted my time in a state of torpor, chasing fantasies of the outside world and running around here and there like an animal, pulled in every direction by my physical needs, obsessed with eating well or not eating food?" You must all critically reexamine how you spent your time here.

In order to arrive at the state where you are unaware of even seeing or hearing, you must be completely immersed in your single-minded questioning of your hwadu, whether sitting or sleeping, walking or talking.

If you have not reached this level, the only possible explanation is your lack of resolve to walk the path of truth. You should be ashamed. Bear in mind that great aspiration and fierce courage must be aroused in order to shatter your hwadu. Have it firmly branded in your mind that until the hwadu is shattered, this retreat never truly ends. If your mind is already wandering towards the frivolous pursuits of the world outside because retreat has ended, or if you are letting your mind wander even during this Dharma talk, that is a disgrace for a practitioner! How can you ever be free from the pull of the three poisons and repay the generosity of your patrons?

Therefore, I ask you not to concern yourself with whether the retreat is over or not. Simply focus with utmost sincerity and effort on the hwadu:

What is my true self from before I was born?

Repeat it thousands or even tens of thousands of times every day if you have to. Eventually, you will generate unceasing doubt so true and powerful that you will spontaneously enter into samadhi.

Mazu Daoyi renounced the world and practiced under the guidance of Seon Master Nanyue Huairang and his sangha. One day when Daoyi was sitting in meditation, Master Huairang asked him, "What are you doing?"

"I am meditating," Mazu responded.

Then the master brought out a roof tile and began to grind it. Mazu asked, "Master, what are you doing?"

"I am trying to make a mirror out of this roof tile."

"But how can you possibly make a mirror out of a tile?"

The master responded, "How will you be awakened by simply sitting in meditation?"

"Then what am I to do, Master?" Mazu asked.

"When the wagon stands still and does not budge, is it right to thrash the wheel, or should you thrash the ox?"

With those words, Mazu had a great awakening.

One day, Master Mazu was passing through a remote mountain field with his attendant Huaihai. Upon reaching a large expanse of farmland, a flock of ducks flew away upon sensing their approach.

At that moment, Master Mazu asked, "What are those that fly away?"

"They are wild ducks, Master."

"Where are they flying?"

"They are flying over to the other side of the mountain, Master."

Upon hearing this reply, Mazu took hold of the attendant's nose and pinched it hard.

"Ouch!" the attendant shouted.

Upon hearing this, Mazu said, "How could it have been flying?"

After taking care of the day's business, Huaihai returned to the temple with his master and went back to his living quarters, locking the door behind him.

When Master Mazu asked, "Where are they flying?" and the attendant answered, "They are flying over the mountain to the other side," why did the master then pinch his nose?

Huaihai started practicing fervently on this hwadu. After questioning it deeply for seven days, completely absorbed in profound samadhi, he shattered the hwadu. Then, he went to Mazu and shouted outside the master's room, "Master, my nose was in pain until last night, but it no longer feels painful today."

Then Mazu called another attendant to ring the bell and summon the assembly.

The whole assembly gathered in the Dharma Hall. While the master ascended the Dharma seat, readying himself to give a talk, Huaihai entered the hall, offered three prostrations, and then rolled up the mat designated for senior monks, put it on his shoulder, and left the hall. At this, Mazu descended from the Dharma seat and returned to his living quarters.

We must understand the place of truth from where this Dharma exchange comes.

What is the meaning of Huaihai's offering three bows and leaving the hall with the mat on his shoulder? And what is the meaning of Master Mazu's descending the Dharma seat and returning to his room, even though he was seated on the Dharma throne and about to give a Dharma talk? If we attain the truth of Seon practice, we will develop the wisdom eye that can correctly discern such meanings effortlessly.

Now, this mountain monk will offer the teachings of the buddhaDharma by examining the truth of the Dharma exchange between these two Seon masters.

When the king rises to the dragon throne and unfurls his sleeves,
The whole is revealed,
And Mt. Sumeru is suspended upside down in thin air.

Huaihai went to practice on other mountains; he returned to Master Mazu after several decades. When Huaihai entered the room where the master was practicing, Master Mazu took the whisk hanging from the corner of the desk and held it up.

Huaihai asked, "Are you using it as it is, or are you doing without it?" At this, Master Mazu hung the whisk back on the desk.

Master Mazu asked Huaihai, "How are you going to open those two lips and save all sentient beings?"

Huaihai responded by lifting the whisk from the corner of the desk.

Master Mazu asked, "Are you using it as it is, or are you doing without it?" At that very moment when Huaihai was about to return the whisk back to the corner, as Master Mazu had done earlier, Master Mazu bellowed a thunderous, "AUUK!³"

Huaihai lost consciousness for three days from his master's shout.

If we examine the process of Huaihai's enlightenment—specifically, how it arose interdependently as a result of causes and conditions—we can see that Huaihai believed he had attained full realization with his first awakening. Convinced that he had done all he had to do, he moved on to other mountains to reside. But a few decades later, when he returned and engaged in a Seon exchange with his master, Huaihai was completely immobilized by his master's deafening roar.

It is only through such a profound realization that we can achieve life in death, attain the eye to see the supreme truth, and finally finish all our work. Seeing one's true nature is in no way an easy matter.

You must pursue the wisdom eye of past Seon masters and aspire to attain it. Only after you perfect your practice according to this standard can you prevent thousands of men from going blind. Otherwise, you will be responsible for the blindness of tens of thousands, and you will tumble into hell as quickly as an arrow shot from a bow.

---

3 喝: A shout enlightened Seon masters use to teach and test their desciples. In Japanese Zen, it is often referred to as "KATSU!"

This is why the Buddha stressed in no uncertain terms, "To claim that one has attained the path of truth without the guidance of an enlightened master is a sure way of becoming a mara and a nonbeliever."

To attain the boundless world of truth on one's own is impossible. One must meet a bright-eyed enlightened master and be trained, melted down, and reshaped by him hundreds of times in order to become a block of pure gold, completely free from any flaw or stain, immutable for thousands of years. Only then is one ready to proclaim and transmit the world of Buddha's enlightened truth to all beings for ages to come. The Buddha's heart seal was created to enable this transmission.

Buddhism is a religion that searches for enlightenment. Without attaining enlightenment, one can never fathom the world of truth. Therefore, everyone in this assembly must reflect back on the last three months spent wrestling with their hwadu to see whether a pure, sincere and flowing doubt has truly arisen in their heart. If you lack such conviction, think back on the very first moment you aspired to attain enlightenment. A single-minded samadhi, focused purely on the questioning of a hwadu, must flow unceasingly for three months, to the point where you forget the passage of time. Only then will you have the opportunity to attain enlightenment.

Do you understand what the dialogue between father and son, between Masters Mazu and Baizhang, comes down to?

If you do, you are one with all buddhas and patriarchs.

Thirty blows with this Dharma staff are well deserved.

Who do you think should receive the blow, Mazu or Baizhang?

Kicking the Bottle, Standing Straight

September 30, 2012, at Donghwa-sa

Why would I beat them with the Dharma staff? Here lies the great meaning.

Alas! The one word of truth,
Already perfect before even opening the mouth,
Has little use for thinking or discussing, and
Cannot be delivered by all the sages of the past, present, and future.
If people perceive the truth as it really is,
All the karma of many lives will be instantly and
Irrevocably eradicated.

The great Seon Master Baizhang lived in China, where he led an assembly of practitioners several hundred strong.

One day, a feng shui adept came to see Master Baizhang and said, "I found an auspicious site with superior energy on Mt. Dawuishan. Please name a master who will claim this site as his own."

Master Baizhang first volunteered himself, but the feng shui master said no. "Your facial features indicate otherwise. The site has the potential to host a sangha 1,500 strong. One must have the virtuous complexion that can command such a big crowd."

"Then today I will pick out a monk with the wisdom eye who befits such a responsibility from among my assembly." Master Baizhang rang the bell and summoned everyone. He mounted the Dharma seat and announced, "Today, I will select from among you the new master of Mt. Dawuishan. Anyone who gives me the correct answer today will be the head of the new sangha there." He placed a glass bottle on the ground and shouted, "Speak!"

The head monk stood up and replied, "It cannot be called a wooden pillow." Basically, he was saying a glass bottle is a glass bottle. However, Master Baizhang said, "Not correct! Who else will give me an answer?"

Master Wuishan came forward, kicked the bottle, and returned to his seat. Master Baizhang nodded his approval and appointed him as the master of Mt. Dawuishan.

Master Wuishan went to the mountain and spent ten years there, but not a single practitioner appeared. He gave up, thinking, "This mountain is not meant for me." When he packed up his traveling sack and climbed down the mountain, a swarm of wild animals rushed in out of nowhere and blocked his departure. Master Wuishan realized that his time had finally come, and returned to his dwelling. Soon, people flocked to Mt. Dawuishan. Under the master's tutelage, the monastic community grew to be 1500 strong.

One day, Master Wuishan ascended the Dharma seat and addressed the assembly:

One hundred years from now, at a patron's household in the village down the mountain, this mountain monk will be born in the body of a female buffalo. The female buffalo will bear on its right side a brand reading "the monk named Lingyu from Mt. Wuishan." When that time comes, what should we call the female buffalo? Should it be called a female buffalo, or by its name from the previous life, "the monk named Lingyu from Mt. Weishan?"

A monk named Yangshan stepped forward, prostrated himself three times and walked back to his place in the assembly. Delighted, Master Wuishan nodded his approval and said, "Right, right."

Do you understand the father and son of Mt. Wuishan, Masters Wuishan and Yangshan?

The father and the son of Mt. Wuishan,
Proficient at transcending and transforming,

Speak with wondrous capacity,
While perfectly unfettered in silence.

If this mountain monk could be present at the Dharma exchange between this teacher and disciple,

I would whack each of them with one blow from this Dharma staff.

Seon adepts throughout all ages have their eyes open to the truth thanks to their noble teaching. Then, why would I beat them with the Dharma staff? Here lies the great meaning.

One day, Master Wuishan ran into Seon Master Yangshan, who was coming back carrying a spade. Wuishan asked him, "What were you doing with the spade?"

"I am coming back after cutting grass at a field near Mt. Namsan."

"How many of the sangha members joined in cutting grass?"

Yangshan stuck the spade into the ground, placed his hands against the chest respectfully, and stood straight.

Wuishan commented, "Many participated." At this, Yangshan lowered his hands, picked up the spade, and returned to his quarters.

Do you understand the meaning of Yangshan's standing straight with his hands on his chest when asked, "How many of our sangha members joined you?" Were it not for Master Wuishan, Master Yangshan's efforts would have gone unrecognized. Now, do you understand the Dharma exchange between these two masters?

Two masters pluck the stringless zither,
Impregnating the world with exquisite music.

Eloquent Command of This One Phrase

1982 winter retreat at Naewon-sa

If a person fails to display an eloquent command of this one phrase,
he has no business guiding sentient beings on the path.

This singular phrase of truth appears in a flash,
When supreme spiritual faculty manifests itself!
This is treasured above all else.
If this single protean phrase does not arrive lightning-quick,
All is in vain.

Venerable Chan adepts of Tang China, such as Masters Zhaozhou, Yunmen, Linji and Deshan, are revered because they possessed such sublime faculties and penetrating wisdom. Through intellectual deliberation over time one can become an expert at fluently manipulating the various literary genres of the Seon Buddhist tradition—prose, verse, the citing and analysis of precedents and commentary. But spontaneous face-to-face exchange cannot be fabricated through discriminative understanding.

Therefore, if a person fails to display an eloquent command of this one phrase, perfectly and effortlessly, he has no business guiding sentient beings on the path. Furthermore, all that such a person can teach are ignorant views, harmful and dangerous to the world; the numinous state of mind that ancient sages attained is completely beyond such a person's grasp, even in dreams. Many so-called teachers, admired by all as enlightened, often hesitate when faced with this pivotal moment of Dharma exchange because they have neither attained the correct views nor cultivated the mind-ground of the ancient sages.

The truth of the unfathomably boundless buddhaDharma can be digested only if each and every teaching of all the past masters is correctly studied and understood. It is simply unthinkable that their spiritual practice differs from ours. To see one's true nature is to realize the mind; in an enlightened mind, how can their distinctions and ours differ? If there is any difference, it can mean only one thing: that the wisdom eye of either party is not fully open.

Countless masters have spread before us a sumptuous feast of gongans (J. koan) by defeating and shattering all obstacles. Those gongans are the result of their enlightened minds flowing into an infinite number of manifestations, unapproachable by cunning and craftiness, and unobtainable by discursive knowledge and intellectual thinking.

Unless the world of truth opens wide and you achieve infallible certainty through all those gongans, you cannot hope to either embrace the vast resting ground the past masters cultivated or attain the lofty state of mind they realized. Therefore, the practice of all true spiritual seekers must be firmly rooted in the fruits of Dharma reaped in the past, completely penetrating the infinitely overlapping and interwoven net of gongans.

Once upon a time, a monk named Panshan Baoji aroused an extraordinary aspiration and poured all his energies into his practice. After finishing one three-month retreat, he headed to another monastery, mindful of every step he took so as not to lose focus of his hwadu. He was passing by a marketplace when, by chance, he overheard a conversation between a butcher and a customer.

The customer said, "Cut me a pound of clean meat."

The butcher put down his cleaver, put his hands against his chest respectfully and asked, "What meat here is not clean?"

Upon hearing this, Baoji's mind opened four-fifths of the way.

Despite this enlightening encounter, he still could not answer the gongans given by the buddhas and patriarchs correctly and lightning-quick, so he had to continue toiling along onerously.

Then, one day, he was skirting a village when he chanced upon a funeral procession. One of the pallbearers carrying the bier led the lamentation as a cantor, chanting, "The red wheel in the heavens rolls downward to the west, but where does the soul return today?" All the mourners joined in on the chorus, wailing loudly, "Heavens!"

As the lamentation of the mourners brushed by his ears, Panshan Baoji's mind was thoroughly penetrated and perfectly awakened. He went straight to see Master Mazu. They engaged in Seon exchange and their minds connected in Dharma. Baoji became Master Mazu's disciple.

Do you understand? What is the state of mind like upon hearing the wailing of the mourners compared to the state of mind in front of the butcher's?

Those with the correct wisdom eye will surely be able to illuminate these states of mind using wise discernment.

After he attained great awakening, Master Panshan Baoji proclaimed to the assembly:

> The one path toward the upward truth
> Is not known even by a thousand saints.
> Futile bickering by scholars is likened to monkeys
> Trying to grasp the reflection of the moon on the pond.

Such words of wisdom and insight can only be born out of enlightenment. Until the one path toward the upward truth is realized, until one spontaneously produces the singular phrase that opens people's minds at the pivotal moment of Dharma exchange, one is still at a crossroads. Only then can he or she stand shoulder to shoulder with all patriarchs, joining the ranks of all buddhas.

What do you think of the singular phrase that contains the cardinal truth?

The moon of the last autumn
Finally falls into the stream ahead, swirling and sloshing.

On the Tip of Each Blade of Grass

January 1, 2011, at Donghwa-sa

*Although the two answers sound identical, the difference is as wide
as the distance between Heaven and Earth.*

Autumn winds sweep through the land,
Mountains and fields sway.
The moon stumbles down into the pond,
Yet the water stays calm.
Roll the jade, roll the foundation of truth.
***"Hahaha"*—the sound of laughter.**
Immediate is their encounter;
They do not recognize each other.

Layman Pang of Tang China is perhaps the greatest of all householder
sages born since Seon teachings of Buddha first emerged. Countless
non-monastic seekers, both male and female, attained enlightenment by
learning Seon, the loftiest of all teachings, but no one has surpassed the
clarity of the Seon eye that Layman Pang accomplished.

Layman Pang, led by Seon Masters Mazu and Shitou—the two
preeminent Chinese masters of his time—lived during the golden age
of Chan in the Tang Dynasty. Virtuous and courageous monks and lay
practitioners alike flocked to the masters' sides to receive training and

guidance. One day, drawing from the depth of his faith, Layman Pang mustered up courage and went to see Master Shitou. He supplicated by way of three bows and asked the master a noble question: "What kind of man is he who is not a companion to the ten thousand Dharmas?"

In reply, Seon Master Shitou placed his hands on Layman Pang's mouth and clamped it shut. Layman Pang's mind suddenly brightened, and it opened about four-fifths of the way.

"Master, thank you so much." Layman Pang prostrated to Master Shitou in farewell and in gratitude, then walked hundreds of miles to meet Master Mazu.

After again offering three deep bows, Layman Pang repeated his question: "What kind of man is he who is not a companion to the ten thousand Dharmas?" Master Mazu answered, "I will tell you after you have swallowed the entire West River in one gulp."

At these marvelous words, Layman Pang's mind completely opened, filling with the radiant light of enlightenment. As he gained the supreme truth of Seon, equal to all the buddhas and patriarchs, Layman Pang became Master Mazu's disciple.

Upon returning home, he gave away all his family wealth and treasures to the neighbors. After that, he and his wife and their daughter lived a simple life in a small thatched hut near a river. They concentrated on the practice of Seon, supporting themselves by making bamboo utensils. The daughter, whose name was Lingzhou, never married. In time, the eyes of the whole family were opened to the truth of the buddhaDharma.

One day, Layman Pang decided to test his daughter's attainment. He said to her, "On the tip of each blade of grass rests the dazzling truth of the Buddha." Lingzhou retorted back immediately, "Your hair turned white and your teeth yellowed from protracted practice. Is this the only opinion you can manage?"

People in the secular world may scold her for her impertinence, but among enlightened beings, all are equal in discussing the highest form of Dharma.

Layman Pang then questioned his daughter, "So what is your opinion?"

She replied, "On the tip of each blade of grass rests the dazzling truth of the Buddha."

The daughter came up with a rejoinder the same as her father's—thus demonstrating how formidable was her mind. Although the two answers sound identical, the difference is as wide as the distance between Heaven and Earth.

From time immemorial, the truth of buddhaDharma has resided in radiant-eyed insight, never in a hairstyle or in particular clothes. If one is awakened to this truth, the distinction between laity and monastic holds no relevance.

As the rumors about Layman Pang's family grew, many practitioners came to witness the wonders of a whole family living in fulfillment of their true nature. One day, when Lingzhou was washing vegetables near the well, Seon Master Danxia Tianran came to visit Layman Pang. He asked her, "Is Layman Pang home?" Lingzhou stopped what she was doing, placed her palms against her chest respectfully, and stood still.

The Master understood her meaning right away, but to test Lingzhou, he asked again, "Is Layman Pang home?" She answered by putting her hands down, then picked up the basket containing vegetables and went into the hut." Master Tianran turned back and left at once.

Words are loud and clear in the absence of speech. Unless our ears are attuned to such words, we cannot aspire to noble expression.

The profound depth of wisdom manifested in this exchange proves that the true peerless beauty of the Tang Dynasty was not Yang Kuei-Fei but Lingzhou. By displaying the majesty of the penetrating wisdom of all buddhas and enlightened sages, she earned an exalted place in their ranks.

One day, Layman Pang was resting at home with his family. He suddenly mumbled to his wife, "Difficult! Difficult! It is like smearing the top of a tall tree with a bushel of oil." His wife retorted, "Easy! Easy! The truth of buddhaDharma is reflected on the tip of every blade of glass."

Now, Lingzhou jumped in like a flash of lightning and said, "It's not difficult, and it's not easy. When I'm thirsty, I drink tea. When I'm tired, I sleep."

What a great family, what great *upasaka*[4] and *upasika*[5], each equipped with the wisdom eye of all buddhas and enlightened beings, with no

---

4 Male lay Buddhist

5 Female lay Buddhist

difference even by the breadth of a hair!

One day, Layman Pang was sitting in meditation. When Lingzhou entered the room, he said, "I intend to pass away when the sun is directly overhead. Go outside and watch for the moment when noon arrives."

In a few minutes, Lingzhou returned and shouted "Oh, Father! There's been an eclipse—I cannot see the sun!"

"An eclipse? Let me take a look." When Layman Pang rose and went outside, Lingzhou took her father's seat and passed away.

How extraordinary is it?

Layman Pang returned to the room and found his daughter dead. "Oh, wicked girl, she tricked me! But daughter, it is splendidly done!" Pang cried. "I will put off my departure for one week to give her body a proper cremation and a funeral." A week later, he too entered nirvana.

After awhile, an old woman living next door came knocking on their door. When no one answered, she opened the door and found Layman Pang dead sitting upright on his meditation cushion. She ran to the field where Pang's wife was squatting down and picking weeds and told her, "It looks like your husband entered nirvana." At that very moment, his wife calmly shrugged off her body as well, with one hand still grabbing the weed and the other hand holding the hand-hoe.

How confident and cheerful were they? This is indeed the true power of Seon practice. Everyone—and I mean everyone—can live as splendidly, depart as splendidly, and come back as splendidly as Layman Pang's family, if one's eyes are open to the truth through correct practice.

Do you know Layman Pang's family now?

Layman Pang embraced the supreme parinirvana.

Three Slaps

August 2, 1992, at Haeunjeong-sa

A profound truth lies hidden in unmoving quiet.

From those who are blessed with the flawless faculty of
The loftiest truth,
All buddhas and patriarchs have nowhere to hide;
Even the lightning has to turn tail and race from
The flash of sweeping and unimpeded function.

Do you understand?

Peach blossoms are pink, the pear blooms white,
And the rose blushes red;
I ask the people in the East, "What does this mean?"
But they do not know.

It is very difficult to understand this type of teaching correctly. But if you attain its true meaning right away, right here, you will enter a sphere where all the buddhas attain the life and comforts of the body. All the myriad Dharma teachings will be made perfectly clear and will be at your fingertips, without restrictions. You will manifest yourself as an ordinary being if an ordinary being comes to you, and manifest yourself as a sage if a sage comes to you, so that you can involve and inspire them in the Seon quest. If such effortless attunement and engagement are still out of your reach, then that means the gates to the great path are not yet fully open to you. If this is the case, return to your hwadu, again and again.

A study of our Linji lineage reveals such illustrious names as Baizhang, a Dharma successor of Mazu, and Huangbo, the teacher of Linji. All achieved unsurpassed supreme enlightenment, complete with consummate insight.

One day, Huangbo went to Seon Master Baizhang and asked, "How will you continue to offer the cardinal teaching of Mahayana tradition and unsurpassed supreme truth?" But Master Baizhang remained seated in silence. A profound truth lies hidden in this unmoving quiet. Then, Huangbo spoke again, "It is not fair to let posterity struggle, despondent and unconnected." To this Master Baizhang responded by saying, "In this case, you are the person in question," and retreated into his room.

Why did Seon Master Baizhang refer to Huangbo as the "person in question?" This reference is also replete with great meaning, that he transmitted the Dharma seal to Huangbo. We must develop the eye of wisdom that can immediately recognize the truth of this teaching. If you do, you will avoid being born into the three lower realms life after life, incarnation after incarnation; you will glory in the bliss of the truth and delight in the sublime joys of nirvana for eternity.

Master Huangbo was born in the golden age of Chan in Tang China, an era that witnessed a great flourishing of Buddhism led by many esteemed masters. Xianzong, the emperor at that time, had two sons, both of whom eventually became emperors themselves. The elder of the two was Emperor Muzong, whose three sons became Emperors Jingzong, Wenzong, and Wuzong.

During the reign of Emperor Muzong—when his younger brother Dazhong, who later became Emperor Xuanzong, was ten years old—Dazhong would observe the emperor closely while he discussed national affairs with government bureaucrats. Later, he would sneak into the audience chamber and hold a mock court with other children, mimicking the discussion with ministers while seated on the dragon throne. He did this often enough to alarm the courtiers who warned the emperor, "Your brother's mimicry must mirror a secret desire lurking in his heart. You must take precautions." Emperor Muzong went to his brother, patted his head and praised him. "What an exceptionally bright child you are. I am proud of you!"

Emperor Muzong passed away, and his three sons succeeded him, one after the other. When the youngest of the three became Emperor Wuzong, he enslaved Dazhong and later tried to put him to death for insulting the late Emperor Muzong by playing on the sacred throne when Dazhong was young. The emperor instructed one of his men to beat Dazhong to death in the backyard of the palace. When Dazhong lost consciousness, the henchman mistook him for being dead, covered Dazhong's body with the straw mat, and left the scene. But Dazhong managed to survive the attack. He escaped to the mountains at night and joined Master Xingyan Zhixian's sangha as a novice monk.

One day, Master Xingyan and the novice monk Dazhong went to see a waterfall on Mt. Lushan. Facing the awe-inspiring spectacle of torrents of water gushing down from a dizzying height into the gorge, Master Xingyan composed a poem.

> Through the cloud, through the rocks, the water penetrates all with ease.
> It flows from a far, faraway origin, and falls from a fathomless height.

There, Master Xingyan stopped and ordered Dazhong to complete the last two lines to assess his character. Dazhong eagerly accepted and finished the poem without hesitation.

> How can it stay stale in a small brook in a mountain valley?
> It will return to the ocean and churn up rolling ripples.

Hearing this, Master Xingyan slapped his knee and said, "That is it! Just be patient and wait for your time." The master had seen through his disguise and recognized that he was destined to go back to the world and create big waves. Novice monk Dazhong then proceeded to join Master Yanguan's sangha, where Master Huangbo was serving as the senior disciplinary monk, and he waited.

The monastic community offers a prayer service three times a day: at dawn, in the late morning, and in the evening. One day, Dazhong approached Master Huangbo, who was leading the ceremony, and asked, "The Buddha stated, 'Do not crave nor seek the Buddha; do not crave nor seek the Dharma of truth; do not crave nor seek the monastic sangha.' So why do monks offer prayer services every day to the image of the Buddha?"

Master Huangbo answered, "One prays to the Buddha neither craving nor seeking the Buddha; one prays to the Dharma without craving nor seeking the Dharma of truth; one prays to the masters neither craving nor seeking the monastic sangha." Dazhong retorted, "If so, then there is no need for the ceremony at all, is there?" Master Huangbo responded by slapping his face. Dazhong continued, saying, "What a coarse and crass monk you are!" The master exclaimed, "How can there be such a distinction between coarse and refined in the truth of the Buddha?" and slapped him twice more.

Eventually, Dazhong was crowned Emperor Xuanzong. After he returned to the court, he remembered those three slaps from Master Huangbo and decided to give him the nickname "Mendicant Monk of Crude and Crass Conduct." However, a nobleman named Peixiu stepped forward and counseled against it. Peixiu was a devout Buddhist and ardent Chan practitioner who had studied under Master Huangbo all his life. Graced with the wisdom that recognized the truth, Peixiu became quite an adept later in his life, even requesting the transmission of the Dharma seal from Master Huangbo. At that time, Peixiu held the position of Grand Chancellor in the Tang Chinese government, equivalent to a prime minister today. Therefore, he advised against the emperor's attempt to humiliate Master Huangbo.

"Your Majesty, I beseech you to rescind your order. It was the three slaps you received from Master Huangbo that cancelled out all your bad karma of the past, present, and future. They paved the way to your imperial reign today."

Emperor Xuanzong was a sincere Buddhist after all. He realized that Peixiu's counsel was true, and thus he conferred the title "Zen Master Who Destroys All Karma of Three Ages" on Master Huangbo and revered him as a great Chan master.

In the same way, the Dharma staff of a truly enlightened teacher will wipe out the immeasurable karma of sentient beings with one whack. Likewise, a single phrase of the truth from their mouths, even if it just brushes against the ear and disappears, will wipe out countless bad habits acquired through endless eons. If this one phrase of truth is to be firmly branded in your mind, you will attain the wisdom of the true awakening of the Buddha.

You should appreciate how sacred this Dharma assembly is. No matter how fabulous and grand secular affairs appear to be, nothing in this world surpasses the noble work of purging the myriad defilements that take hold in the mind.

What, then, would be the final word of truth?

Chanting the song of truth, one hymn after another,
But no one embraces it.
Range after range of blue mountains bursting through
The boundless ocean of cloud.

Begging Bowls

1991 seven-day intensive meditation retreat at Haeunjeong-sa

If any of you truly understands the meaning,
I will humbly offer you this Dharma staff.

It stands on its own without being supported;
It soars without being lifted.
Only if the wisdom's foundation frees itself from
The desolate and dangerous
Will the sublime and mystical be seen.

Which sages have lived such unhindered lives?

Seon Master Deshan, along with Seon Master Linji, is legendary even among the patriarchs for fearlessly showing the world the highest Dharma. He had two outstanding disciples, Yantou and Xuefeng.

One day, when the meal was not served on time, Master Deshan came to the dining hall carrying his alms bowls. Xuefeng, who was in charge of cooking the meals in the kitchen, saw the master and asked, "Where are you going with your alms bowls when the bell has not yet been rung or the drum struck?" Hearing this, Master Deshan hung his head and returned to his room in silence. When Xuefeng relayed the story to Yantou, Deshan's senior disciple, Yantou cockily replied, "The pathetic old teacher does not know the final phrase of the supreme truth."

Yantou's remark caused quite a stir in the assembly. Master Deshan summoned and admonished Yantou. "Why did you say that I did not know the final phrase of the supreme truth?" Yantou whispered secretly into Master Deshan's ear what his comment had meant.

The next day, Deshan gave an extraordinary Dharma talk, completely unlike any of his past teachings. When the master finished and dismounted the Dharma seat, Yantou, still rejoicing at the talk, held the master's hands and said, "Now that the master has attained the final phrase of the supreme truth, your lofty Dharma will be unsurpassed for ages to come. Unfortunately, your life will come to an end in a mere three years." And in fact, Master Deshan entered parinirvana just after three years had passed.

This story of "Deshan coming out with his begging bowls" has been the subject of heated debate in the Chinese sangha for a long time. It is a teaching of such deep insight and profound truth that it was often incomprehensible even to many masters of sterling reputation. They found themselves thrown off guard, flustered and confused by it. As such, in China, only masters who attained truly bright wisdom eyes were able to engage in Seon exchanges based on this gongan. Those who are shallow in attainment will not even dare to mention it.

It has been over six hundred years since the path of Seon was introduced into Korea, but this particular gongan was almost never used to teach and test a monastic assembly until Masters Hyanggok and Seongcheol finally applied it to Seon exchanges and dialogues, attesting to the exalted nature of the teaching this gongan conveys.

If any of you truly understands the meaning of why Master Deshan returned to his room with his head down, and the truth of Yantou's whispering into his ear, I will humbly offer you this Dharma staff and confer on you the title of Mt. Jangsu's second master today.

I ask again: Do you understand why, after Xuefeng asked him where he was going with his bowls when the bell had not yet sounded, Seon Master Deshan bent his head low and returned to his room?

Once, a monk named Mingzhao came forward and said, "If I were there, I would have said, 'It is heartbreakingly regrettable. There is nowhere else to go!' " After making this assertion, Mingzhao was severely scolded by Seon Master Xuedou: "Mingzhao was widely reputed to have the eyes of a dragon, yet he turned out to have only one eye! He did not know Master Deshan was a toothless tiger."

When this mountain monk was studying under Seon Master Hyanggok in Myogwaneum-sa Monastery, the master brought up this gongan and said, "Master Xuedou harshly reprimanded Venerable Mingzhao for falsely examining the ancient sage's wisdom eye. How do you answer if I ask you the meaning of Seon Master Deshan's returning to his room with his head bent low?"

This mountain monk replied, "Convenience is lost when it is gained."

With regard to the gongan involving Yantou, who had whispered to Master Deshan, Seon Master Hyanggok had publicly challenged the masters all around the country to reply to this gongan appropriately. All he heard then was absurd gibberish and lame nonsense, such as "I will be hit with a cudgel." So Master Hyanggok presented this gongan to me again and asked if I understood its true meaning. This mountain monk then answered:

**Mazu trampled the world and crushed everyone under heaven,
But Linji has yet to be the villain who masterfully steals and
Cheats in broad daylight.**

The master found my reply satisfactory.

A Foot in the Doorway

November 28, 2012, at Donghwa-sa

Where can you find the place where one hand is raised
and the other hand is dropped?

A wailing lamentation for the dead does not pierce the heart,
Nor does roaring laughter lighten it.
Flipping the stomach and flicking the intestine,
I tell you this:
The father and the son are not close—Are you aware of this or not?
Three pounds of iron falls on the back of your head
The moment you lift it.

Today marks the beginning of the winter retreat. Everyone from the fourfold community must grapple diligently with his or her hwadu in everyday life, so as to attain one-mindedness through the doubt generated by questioning a hwadu. If you do not have a hwadu yet, then choose this as your hwadu now:

What is my true self from before I was born?

Hold this hwadu at all times, awake or asleep, fervently investigating and doubting until all distracting and useless thoughts vanish, and the intense doubt generated by the hwadu flows unceasingly like a torrent of water. One should become oblivious to the passage of day and night, disregarding how many days or even months have gone by, and forget even the sense of seeing or hearing. Then, suddenly, eyes open upon seeing an object, and ears open upon hearing a sound. In a single instant, the hwadu is thus shattered. Then, one attains the Buddha's world of truth, the original home of mind, without moving a single step; one stands shoulder to shoulder with all the buddhas and patriarchs, sharing the glories of a fearless hero.

This mountain monk adds just another word lamenting the reality of the garden of patriarchs:

There remain the teachings of Seon, but alas,
There are no more truly enlightened teachers,
Leaving the lantern in the garden of Seon
Dangerously exposed to the gusts of wind and heavy rain.
Woe is me!
I grieve those who follow only words
In the Four Seas and Five Lakes!
Stop mimicking Dharma talks of enlightened teachers—
You must reach deep down into your own heart and heave up
The one phrase of supreme truth that covers Heaven and Earth.

Long ago, a Seon Master named Yantou was born with the eye of wisdom, already a learned being at birth. He served Seon Master Deshan as his attendant. One day, he went to Master Deshan's room, opened the door, and with one foot in and the other still left outside, asked, "Master, am I an enlightened sage or an ordinary ignorant being?" Master Deshan only gave a thundering roar, "AAUUK!" Hearing this, Master Yantou prostrated himself once and left.

Later, when Master Dongshan heard of the exchange between Deshan and Yantou, he commented, "Had it not been for Yantou, Deshan's roar would have been difficult to understand." Yantou was informed of Dongshan's comment and remarked, "The old man Dongshan talks wildly without knowing what is good and bad. At that time, I raised one hand

and dropped the other."

Where can you find the place where one hand is raised and the other hand is dropped?

If we fail to awaken to the true nature of reality in this life, then when will we ever have the extreme good fortune to encounter the Dharma again? We wander astray over countless eons of cyclical births and deaths and finally manifest in a human body and are introduced to the buddhaDharma in this life; it would be utterly useless to regret not attaining enlightenment while on your death bed, having succumbed to sloth and procrastination. It is difficult to be blessed with rebirth as a human; it is even more so to be granted with an opportunity to study the truth of awakening. If one listens to the correct teachings of a clear-eyed master and sincerely aspires to be awakened to one's own true nature, then Seon practice will, without fail, bring good news and welcome results. Do whatever it takes and pour your body and soul into attaining one-mindedness within the next three months.

If you want to greet Master Yantou in person, know this:

It would be impossible at the lofty peak of Mt. Myobong,
But you will see him at a different peak.

Thunderous Roar, Crushing Blows

End of 2011 winter retreat at Donghwa-sa

Keep doubting until the process seeps into the very marrow of your bones.

Linji's roar and Deshan's blow are
The golden rules of the Seon patriarchal lineage,
While Zhaozhou greets both enlightened saints and
Ordinary sentient beings with a cup of tea.
So, which is correct? The golden rules of the Seon lineage,
Or Zhaozhou's cup of tea for all?

The bitterest cold of the winter solstice will pass
After forty-five days, heralding the first day of spring.

Time indeed flies—today marks the end of yet another three-month retreat. The retreat may have come to an end, but practice never does. We are all alive today, but tomorrow is guaranteed to no one. You should search your soul every day and ask yourself: "How was my practice today? How diligent was my effort, and how heartfelt was my hwadu investigation?" You must be sure that the doubt generated by your hwadu flows pure and bright today; otherwise, if you die tomorrow, you will be dragged off to the underworld and tortured by King Yama. Dozens or even hundreds of lifetimes may be wasted in captivity before you once again encounter the supreme teachings of the Buddha that can awaken you to your true nature.

You must complete this great mission by any means necessary in this life, before you discard this body. If you do not, you are at risk of spending an extended sojourn in the realm of hell, or of being reborn as a cow or a horse in the animal realm. You must understand how rare it is to be presented all the right causes and conditions needed to encounter the Dharma in one lifetime; let this understanding compel you to never waste time.

Buddhas cannot find your true nature for you. Numerous teachings from an enlightened teacher can never be a substitute for sincere practice. The only reason you are distracted by pointless thoughts, are disturbed by delusions, or have your practice derailed by torpor is that your questioning is not desperate enough to penetrate to the bone. Once you have received the correct guidance, patiently stay on the correct path. When your hwadu single-mindedness matures and starts flowing unceasingly, then suddenly, without having taken a single step, you will find yourself already inside the gates of truth.

Keep doubting and investigating, whether awake or asleep, standing or sitting, walking or lying down. Keep doubting and investigating until the process seeps into the very marrow of your bones. Once a genuine doubt—a true sense of questioning—is aroused and sustained for a full three months, then anyone can enter the land of all the buddhas and patriarchs and join them in the eternal bliss of nirvana.

The only thing that you need is faith that your unrelenting questioning of hwadu for the next three months will surely bear the ultimate fruit before the summer retreat starts. Marshal all you have into continuing your hwadu investigation.

In the old days, Seon Master Linji bellowed a thunderous "AUUK!" at whomever came to ask for the truth of Buddha. Anyone who sought out Seon Master Deshan would get a beating with his Dharma staff and be driven away.

Master Linji, well-known for his sudden shouts, was the founder of the Linji School of Chan, and Master Deshan, notorious for threatening to beat his students, was one of the most renowned masters of the Caodong lineage. Since the teachings of these two Chan schools are nearly alike, this mountain monk refers to Linji's roar and Deshan's blow as being the golden rules of the Seon lineage. Zhaozhou, meanwhile, served a cup of tea to all enlightened saints and ordinary sentient beings alike.

Master Deshan always said in his Dharma talks, "Speak correctly and you get thirty blows. Speak incorrectly, and you still get thirty blows." When word of his method got around, Master Linji summoned his young attendant and instructed him to go pay a visit to Master Deshan. "Do as I say," he said. "Walk up to him and ask, 'Why do you give them thirty blows when they speak correctly, and still give them thirty blows when they do not?' When he raises his stick to strike you, push him."

The attendant went to see Master Deshan and did as he was told. As expected, Master Deshan raised his staff to hit him, and the attendant shoved the master hard. Since the master was old and frail, he stumbled and fell. Then he stood up and simply returned to his room.

The attendant came back and reported what happened. Master Linji said, "I have always suspected old man Deshan." This means Master Linji either suspected that Master Deshan attained the correct wisdom eye, or that he was a villain with the enlightened eye. It is the enlightened eye that sees the truth of what Master Linji suspected.

When his life drew near its end, after a lifetime of spectacular displays of Seon in its most wondrous forms, Master Linji summoned his disciple, Sansheng Huiran, and tested him: "If you were asked the loftiest meaning of buddhaDharma, how would you answer?" Sansheng bellowed a booming "AUUK!" Master Linji said, "Who would know that the Dharma of Buddha has been slashed clean by this blind donkey?" He passed on the seal of his lineage to Sansheng, then closed his eyes and entered parinirvana.

Sansheng, the heart disciple and Dharma heir of Linji, never established his own Dharma assembly and spent the rest of his life visiting other great masters, engaging in Seon dialogue with them, and quietly practicing with their disciples.

One day, a monk paid a visit to this mountain monk. He was the head of a Seon center and rumored to be enlightened, so I threw him a question by quoting a Dharma exchange between Master Zhaozhou and one of his students:

One day, a monk came to see Zhaozhou after a three-month retreat. With all his possessions packed in a sack slung over his shoulder, he bade farewell to Zhaozhou saying, "I had a good retreat thanks to your teaching and guidance. Now I intend to leave to join another sangha." Zhaozhou told him, "Do not stay where the Buddha resides. Quickly run away from any place the Buddha does not reside as well. While on the run three thousand miles away, if you meet someone, make sure you do not incorrectly convey to him the words just uttered." The monk answered, "If so, I will not go." To this, Zhaozhou responded, "It is plucking the willow leaves and plucking the willow leaves!"

I ask the same question now. Master Zhaozhou said, "It is plucking the willow leaves, and doing it ever again." What do you think of this?

Plucking the willow leaves,
Plucking the willow leaves.
Not even a black stallion that runs a thousand miles a day can follow.

The Ferryman

February 9, 2009, at Haeunjeong-sa

How would you save the child?

The bright light of the New Year's full moon
Reveals all things of the universe in gilded glitter,
While the wisdom moon of a true spiritual seeker's heart
Illuminates all creations of myriad colors and shapes;
But the moon itself is formless, without even a trace.
The sound of waves in Haeundae Sea is the entirety of
Shakyamuni Buddha's forty-nine years of enlightened life,
His boundless teachings.
Who truly understands what profound truth
The Buddha's one phrase lays bare?

There is a wide array of spiritual practices available in Buddhism, but if properly initiated and correctly trained in this life in the Seon practice of the living phrase, anyone can become an enlightened being who has perfected the path; anyone can revel in the exuberance of truth for endless eons. Therefore, everyone should now accept this hwadu:

What is my true self from before I was born?

Hold this hwadu at all times, awake or asleep, fervently investigating and questioning so that the one mind focused only on the hwadu will flow steady and sound.

Seon Master Yantou once disguised himself as a boatman on the bank of a large river. He installed wooden boards on both sides of the river, and when people knocked on the wood, Seon Master Yantou would come out dancing from his hut, his oar on his shoulder, and ferry them across the river.

One day, a middle-aged woman came with a child and asked him to ferry them across. When the boat reached the middle of the river, the woman suddenly grabbed the child and asked Master Yantou, "Where has this child come from?"

Yantou tapped the side of the boat three times with the oar.

The woman lamented, "I was never able to raise my children, even though I gave birth to six of them, because I have yet to meet a person whose eyes are open to the truth. Alas! This seventh child is no exception!" And with that, she threw the child into the river.

How would you answer the woman's question to save the child? Would you understand Master Yantou and the woman?

Two villains steal and cheat each other; it is difficult to tell which one is an elder or a younger brother.

The Cup in Which the Altar Wine Is Served

End of the 1997 summer retreat at Donghwa-sa

> *What compels a man to throw away his robes*
> *and bowl and live the life of a recluse?*

Dharma is so vast that it has no need for any mandate from an emperor consecrated by Heaven;
All sentient beings serenade peace on Earth.

If we could transform all activities of everyday life into occasions for practice, we could live content and carefree as our body and mind grow happy and healthy, liberated from distress and trouble. How, then, do we practice? Keep asking yourself:

What is my true self from before I was born?

Keep asking until such questioning develops into an unceasing flow of single-minded focus on your hwadu. This will lay to rest all the afflictions and anxieties clouding your mind; in their place, a pure and clear mind will slowly settle in and take root.

One of the true disciples of Dongshan Liangjie was Xianzi. After he received the Dharma seal from Seon Master Dongshan, Xianzi flung down his monastic robes and alms bowl, abandoned the precepts, and wandered the world with no fixed home. He sustained himself on shrimp and shellfish he caught on the river bank and slept at night buried in a mound of paper money dedicated to a tomb shrine called the White Horse.

Hearing about Xianzi, Master Huayan Xiujing went to see him. Master Huayan hid himself underneath the pile of paper money, and when Xianzi finally showed up at night, the master suddenly put his arms around Xianzi's waist and, in the pitch darkness, asked him, "What is the meaning of Bodhidharma coming from the west?"

Xianzi answered: "It is the cup in which altar wine is served."

Master Huayan bowed in admiration of Xianzi's wisdom and praised him by saying, "How surprising to find such a lofty and noble eye among the students of Master Dongshan!" Then Master Huayan left.

What an inscrutable mystery Dharma is that it compels a man to throw away his monastic robes and alms bowl and live the life of a recluse!

So, this mountain monk will now ask you: do you know Xianzi?

Myriad buddhas of the past, present, and future are mere figures in a dream.
Spiritual seekers of the Four Seas and Five Lakes!
Drink up a bowl of icy water and lay to rest your delusions.
Who is the most beautiful person in the world?
It is the one who answers, "It is a cup in which altar wine is served."

The Dharma Freely Wielded

October 19, 2012, at Donghwa-sa

You must freely wield Dharma so as not to be dragged off to the underworld.

Abodes of the buddhas and bodhisattvas lie far, far away,
The road to which is filled with the exquisite fragrance of
Plum blossoms every step of the way.
Yet the people of the time are not allowed to view the sweet balm.
It is feared that the spring winds may betray the poignant perfume.

Once long ago, Seon Master Sansheng Huiran was wandering the mountains from one great sangha assembly to another. One such assembly was Seon Master Weishan Lingyu's, where Sansheng stayed for three years in silent retreat. One day, Master Weishan gave instructions and a small stick to his attendant and dispatched him to Master Sansheng.

The attendant came up to Master Sansheng and asked, "Can you lift this stick?" Sansheng replied, "The master of this sangha has business to take care of." When the attendant reported the exchange to Master Weishan, he told the attendant to go back and ask the same question again. The attendant then returned to Master Sansheng and asked again, "Can you lift this stick?" Sansheng replied, "A second violation will not be tolerated."

Upon hearing this magnificent answer, Weishan conferred his seal of approval upon Sansheng.

A few days afterward, Master Sansheng went to see Master Weishan to bid farewell. Master Weishan called his attendant, saying, "Bring my Dharma staff and whisk."

"I already have a teacher," Master Sansheng replied.

"Who is he?"

"Seon Master Linji."

"Linji is lucky to have a disciple such as you."

One day, Master Yangshan Huiji, the heart disciple of Master Weishan, asked Master Sansheng Huiran, "What is your name?"

"Huiji."

"That is my name."

"Yes," said, Sansheng, "my name is Huiran."

What a splendid faculty and manifestation of Dharma! Why did Sansheng say that his name was Huiji when that was in fact Master Yangshan's name? You monks must cultivate such a marvelous capacity to freely wield Dharma so as not to be dragged off to the underworld by King Yama.

One day, Sansheng visited and sought an audience with Master Deshan, who, along with his teacher, Seon Master Linji, was considered one of the two greatest Seon masters of that time. Sansheng was unfolding a cushion to prostrate himself on it when Deshan dismissed him brusquely: "There is no need to bother with the cushion. We don't even have cold rice and congealed soup to spare for the likes of you." Sansheng asked in reply, "Even if you did, where would you put them?" Deshan raised his staff and hit him. In return, Sansheng pushed back, causing Deshan to fall to the floor. Then he helped the old master up and led him to a low wooden bench. Master Deshan clapped and roared in laughter, "Ha! Ha!" while Master Sansheng let out a wailing cry for the dead, "Heavens!" and left.

Do you know what this exchange between Masters Deshan and Sansheng comes down to?

When this mountain monk ransacked Liancheng and
Took all the treasures,
Both the Chin Emperor and Xiang Ru were dead.

The Saintly Trio

April 6, 1993, at Haeunjeong-sa

Bodhisattvas manifest in a multitude of ways.

Claim the truth of this Dharma staff, and
Join the ranks of myriad buddhas.
Claim the truth of this Dharma staff, and
Plunge into hell like an arrow shot from a bow.

Which one of these two would you claim as your aim of practice for enlightenment?

Hanshan and Shide are honored as manifestations of the bodhisattvas Manjusri and Samantabhadra respectively, while Master Fenggan is regarded as the manifestation of Maitreya. All are great bodhisattvas who, for many billions of years, have reincarnated in an infinite variety of forms to teach Dharma and save all beings. This Dharma, once perfectly and truly attained, is eternal. Therefore, the dazzling light of an enlightened mind, even though its presence may not be always recognizable, can never be dimmed but will radiate ever brightly like a sun.

Hanshan and Shide have been reborn as Dharma friends and taught Dharma to sentient beings together in world after world, life after life. One day, Hanshan realized that he had been without Shide's companionship for quite some time, and, with his wisdom eye, saw that Shide had incarnated as a sow and now had a large litter of piglets.

Hanshan wrote Shide a letter saying, "One risks losing sight of the original luminosity of an enlightened mind by abiding too long buried in the dust of samsara. Why don't you return promptly to the green mountain?" He then had a messenger deliver it to the pig.

When the messenger went to the spot on the outskirts of the village as instructed, he found an enormous sow sprawling in a pigsty crowded with piglets. When he threw the letter to the sow, it caught the letter in its mouth, then chewed and swallowed it. Shide then immediately shed his pig incarnation.

Great bodhisattvas manifest in a multitude of ways in order to accommodate and attune themselves to the vast spectrum of sentient beings' karma.

For one lifetime, Hanshan and Shide chose to be at Guoqingsi Monastery on Mt. Tiantai, where they lived among the followers of Master Fenggan. Hanshan, whose name means "Cold Mountain," was so named because he had issued forth from a rock, while Shide was an orphan found abandoned on the road by Master Fenggan. The master brought him back to the monastery and raised him, where he came to be called "Foundling."

One day, when Shide was sweeping the courtyard, the abbot of Guoqingsi Monastery approached him and asked, "You are called 'Foundling' because Master Fenggan found you and brought you here. What was your original last name?"

Shide put down the broom and stood upright respectfully with his hands against this chest. Puzzled, the abbot asked again, "I said, what was your original last name?" Shide picked up the broom, turned around, and left.

Hanshan saw the exchange from afar and started wailing, "Heavens!"

Shide asked Hanshan, "Why are you wailing?"

Hanshan answered, "An eastern householder dies and the western householder mourns."

Thus they strolled away, asking and answering, laughing and weeping.

If one attains the great wisdom of the Buddha innate in all of us, every nook and cranny of the whole universe will be restored and reformed as the Pure Buddhaland, where all the myriad teachings will be at one's fingertips.

When asked by the abbot of Guoqingsi Monastery, "What was your original last name?" Shide lay down the broom and put his hands against his chest respectfully. When asked the same question a second time, he just walked away holding his broom. Assembly, do you understand?

**If one masterfully furls and unfurls
The magnificent display of Dharma,
He will delight in serene joy for endless eons to come,
Without falling into darkness.**

One day Hanshan inquired of Master Fenggan, "How can one make an old mirror shine if the mirror is not polished?"

The master replied, "A chunk of ice does not have an original shape. It is like a monkey attempting to grab the moon reflected on the water."

Hanshan did not find his question answered, so he told the master to address it once more, asking, "It is still not shining. Give it another try."

Master Fenggan snapped back, "Ten thousand virtues have not been brought in. What are you telling me to say?"

This is indeed an exchange that will be shining for all eternity. Today, I will present Master Fenggan's wisdom eye. Do you now understand him?

Master Fenggan possesses a naturally discerning wisdom eye.

Holding Fast at the Door

End of 2012 summer retreat at Donghwa-sa

Only someone who has a fiercely determined mind will be able to awaken.

Originally there is no dust on the old mirror.
It is just that people make it dirty and clean it.

On this old mirror that everyone possesses, not even a single spot of dust can be found. It is just that foolish people make it dirty and clean it over and over again.

If anyone can understand what I mean, their work will be finished and they will enjoy the bliss of truth forever.

Listening to the Dharma, expounding Buddha's highest truth, and practicing Ganhwa Seon—all of this is only for the sake of finding the old mirror that we all possess.

It is already the last day of the summer retreat. You need to reflect on just how sincerely and continuously you held and questioned your hwadu over the last three months. To one who wants to enlighten to the great path, the idea of picking up your sack and leaving the retreat should be a fearful one. If you are continuously moving around and wasting time, awakening to the great path is impossible. Only when you break through your hwadu and receive the Dharma seal from an enlightened teacher should you consider the retreat to be over. Until then, you must make your mind as unmoving as a great boulder. Continually practice, practice, and practice some more.

Every time you move your hand or place your foot down, you must question your hwadu. This question should spring from deep inside your heart like a geyser—wrestle with it until it flows like a running stream.

If you keep trying for this single thought, one of these days the true question will unexpectedly arise. You will forget the senses of seeing and hearing; you will be oblivious as to whether it is day or night. You will not be aware of the weeks or months that pass, and suddenly, at that one instant when you see an object or hear a sound, your hwadu will break open. Like a skewer, you will pierce the one hundred thousand gongans of the buddhas and patriarchs in one moment. In this state, if anyone throws you a question, the correct answer will come out, as quick as a spark, as sudden as lightning. You will embrace and use the truth that is not the slightest bit different from that of the buddhas and patriarchs, and I will hand you this staff, making you the 80th descendent of Buddha's lineage.

Don't even consider whether now is a time of retreat or not. Put all of your mind, all of your effort, into creating this single-minded focus on hwadu.

In ancient China, young Yunmen was a monk with a deep aspiration for awakening. He devoted his life to Seon practice. At that time, the Seon Master Muzhou was a famous teacher whom every practitioner wanted to meet at least once. He lived in a small one-room hermitage with a high wall surrounding it so people could not see inside. The wall had only a small gate on one side. Whenever anyone came to pay their respects, the master would open the door halfway—then, with his towering and powerful build, he would grab the person by the collar and shout, "Speak! Speak!" If the visitor could not answer or stuttered for a reply, he would push them out, causing them to fly head over heels. As such, no one ever managed to have a proper audience with him.

When Yunmen heard Master Muzhou had attained a magnificent wisdom eye, he thought, "I must meet him. I will awaken to the great truth by receiving training and guidance from him." As he knocked on the door, the master opened it halfway, grabbed Yunmen by the collar, and shouted, "Speak! Speak!" Yunmen was startled and didn't know what to say. As usual, the master tossed him backwards, slammed the door in this face, and went back inside. To the one who has awakened, when confronted with this question, the answer comes right out. But to someone who has not seen true self, nothing is clear.

Yunmen tried to meet the master several times, but each time he was turned away. One day he became so desperate that he vowed to himself, "I am going to meet the master today even if it kills me!"

When Yunmen knocked at the small gate, Master Muzhou came to the door, reached out to grab him, and shouted, "Speak!" If Yunmen had given the correct answer, the master would have flung open the gate and welcomed him in, but Yunmen hesitated again. This time, though, since he was ready to risk his life to enter the hermitage, he pushed his leg inside while clinging with all his might to the arm clutching his collar, determined not to be pushed out. The two of them pushed and pulled in this manner for awhile, and finally Master Muzhou slammed the door hard, breaking Yunmen's leg. Yunmen screamed in pain. When he heard himself, his hwadu shattered and his eye completely opened to the truth. Only someone who has given rise to such a fiercely determined mind, like Master Yunmen, will be able to awaken.

Seon Master Yunmen spent the rest of his life partly crippled from this broken leg. He hobbled around China with his attendant, spreading the great Dharma and his tradition.

One day, Master Yunmen visited the monastery of Master Xuefeng, who had a following of 1,500 monks in residence. As Master Yunmen reached the gate, he instructed his attendant, "Go to the master's room and ask the master, 'Master, why is it that you have an iron shackle around your neck all the time?' Insist that these are your own words, regardless of what he says in reply."

The attendant went in front of the master's room and did as he was instructed, asking, "Master, why is it that you have an iron shackle around your neck all the time?"

Master Xuefeng immediately threw the door open, grabbed the attendant by the collar, and shouted, "Speak! Speak!"

The attendant hesitated, so the master let him go, saying, "Those aren't your words."

"No master, they are my words," the attendant insisted.

"Listen here, I know they are not."

The attendant insisted, so the master called the monk in charge of discipline and had him ring the bell and gather the assembly of 1,500 monks together. "Until this rascal tells the truth," he instructed, "hang him upside down from the ceiling and beat him up."

The monks tied the attendant up with a rope and lifted him off the ground. When he was about to be beaten, he finally cried out, "They are not my words!"

"Then whose are they?" the master questioned.

"I am just following the instructions of my master, Master Yunmen," the attendant confessed.

"Where is Master Yunmen right now?"

The attendant pointed and said, "He is right outside the gate."

Master Xuefeng turned to his assembly and announced, "Here comes a great master with the wisdom eye capable of teaching five hundred monks. He is outside the gate. Go and reverently escort him in."

It takes a sage to recognize a sage. When your eye is open to the path, you will be able to determine the degree of someone's attainment by even one word or one action.

When Master Xuefeng heard, "Master, why is it that you have an iron shackle around your neck all the time?" he said, "Here comes a great master with the wisdom eye capable of teaching five hundred monks." If you awaken to the path, you will immediately gain the eye that knows the intended meaning of any question thrown at you.

Long ago, Seon Master Lingshu Rumin led an assembly of several hundred monks at his monastery. But for twenty years, he left the position of head monk open. The monks would ask him, "When will our head monk come?"

He would reply, "He's just been born." Sometime later, he would answer, "He is feeding the ox well." Then, he would say, "He is now practicing diligently." He continued to reply like this for twenty years until one day he said, "The head monk will be coming, so make preparations." All of the monks cleaned the grounds, put on their formal robes, and waited at the gate of the monastery.

When the time came, they saw one monk approaching the gate. It was Master Yunmen who, in his travels, had come to pay respects to Master

Lingshu. Master Lingshu announced to the assembly, "Escort the new head monk in!"

As soon as Master Yunmen took his seat, a monk approached with a sword held over his head. "What are you going to do now?" he threatened, testing the master. Master Yunmen calmly and immediately replied, "Blood is overflowing into Indra's palace in the heavens." The monk put away his sword and bowed to the master.

With the wisdom eye open, regardless of what is asked, the correct answer comes right out. The minute the collar is grabbed, the moment the sword is held over the head, such a person clearly knows the answer. That is how he responded, "Blood is overflowing into Indra's palace in the heavens."

And that is also how, for the twenty years the head monk position was open, the master was able to tell the community about the future head monk: when he was born, how he was practicing, his travels, and when he was coming. If one awakens clearly, then he can see through the past, present, and future. One phrase of truth coming from such a person is worth more than all the gold in the world.

Since meeting this Dharma of seeing one's true nature is so rare, even once in a million lifetimes, it is my wish that you will be able to take all of this to heart and question your hwadu with a single-mindedness that pierces into your bones.

What do you think about the final phrase of truth?

The red fog pierces to the bottom of the ocean,
The bright sun wraps around Mt. Sumeru.

Maitreya's True Face Laid Bare

February 6, 1992, at Haeunjeong-sa

*In the truth of Dharma,
both you and I are already courageous heroes.*

**Maitreya, true Maitreya,
Manifesting in hundreds of billions of incarnations.
He often reveals himself,
But the men of this world do not recognize him.**

Great buddhas and bodhisattvas, despite having attained the highest fruit of enlightenment, have appeared among us in a multitude of emanations because of their solemn vow to forego nirvana until all beings are liberated and not a single soul is left in hell. Maitreya, having realized the great path of the Buddha's truth and having mastered infinite skillful means, has manifested himself in countless shapes and forms to save sentient beings suffering in samsara.

At one time, Maitreya incarnated as Master Budai in China. Budai would not go anywhere without a rough hemp sack slung on his back in which he collected all sorts of junk. He gave up all sense of false decorum and abandoned any pretense of holiness. He would unroll a coarse jute mat in the middle of the marketplace, pour out the entire contents of his sack, and ask the shoppers, "What do we have here?"

When onlookers would not say anything, he would pick up a piece of dried fish and declare, "I brought this straight from Tusita Heaven." Then he would pick up a lump of dried feces and claim, "This is a precious treasure from the inner court of Tusita Palace, where Maitreya dwells and teaches." He would spend a whole day like this, loitering and making a show of useless items.

This may seem like the behavior of a lunatic to ordinary people, but if your eyes are open to the truth, you cannot help but realize that dried feces is indeed an inestimably exquisite gem from Maitreya's innermost palace; in fact, you cannot help but perceive anything and everything as being treasured wonders of the world. Once you have reached such an exalted plane of truth, the whole earth is transformed into gold—the 84,000 defilements are transformed, on their own, into bodhi.

Maitreya had a full and free command of the boundless world of truth. He could manifest in front of tens of thousands of houses simultaneously, with the same sack slung over his shoulder and the same alms bowl in his hand begging for food.

Maitreya laid bare his true face and exposed it day in and day out, but the people of this world, blind to the light of truth, did not see it at all, even when it was right in front of their eyes.

Master Budai spent his whole life in this manner. Then one day, he rolled out a straw mat on a dike in a nameless rice field, lay down, and shrugged off his physical body. Since no one retrieved his corpse, it soon decayed, crawling with tens of thousands of maggots. After some days had passed, the maggots suddenly metamorphosed into tens of thousands of Master Budais and scattered in all directions.

Where does such supernatural power come from?

If we discover our true nature through sincere Seon practice, we will be able to make free use of the power intrinsic to such an unimpeded existence. In the truth of Dharma, both you and I are already courageous heroes of Dharma, and both you and I can become Master Budai.

Another time, Maitreya was reborn as a great Buddhist scholar named Fu Dashi in China's Liang Dynasty.

Emperor Wu of Liang, whose fierce piety earned him the posthumous title "Bodhisattva Emperor," heard of Master Fu's fame and invited him to the court to give a Dharma talk on Buddhist scriptures. Master Fu accepted the invitation and came to the imperial court. However, when he mounted the Dharma seat, Master Fu held up the Dharma staff, drew a circle in the air, and immediately dismounted.

Emperor Wu was at a loss for words. Seeing this, Seon Master Zhigong asked the emperor, "Do you understand the meaning of Fu Dashi's dismounting the Dharma seat after holding up the Dharma staff and drawing a circle in the air?

The emperor replied, "I do not."

Then, Master Zhigong explained, "Fu Dashi is done with his Dharma teaching."

If your eyes are open to the realm of truth, there is no longer any need to expound on every single word and phrase from all the 84,000 scriptures in the Buddhist canon. Every move you make and every step you take is already the turning of the great wheel of Dharma.

Fu Dashi is revered as the manifestation of Maitreya, while Master Zhigong was an incarnation of Avalokitesvara; both came back to this samsaric existence to save sentient beings from suffering. That is why Master Zhigong was immediately able to fathom what Fu Dashi meant by holding up the Dharma staff, drawing a circle in the air, and leaving.

Do you know Fu Dashi?

If this mountain monk examines him carefully,

Fu Dashi gave an excellent Dharma teaching,
But only half of it was delivered.

So what is the final word of truth?

Unable to grab and gain a fistful of willow branches in one's hands,
Leave them hanging in the spring wind on the jade banister.

Circling the Meditation Seat

November 28, 2013, at Donghwa-sa

Even if a fire is set, there will be nothing left to burn.

The golden wind sweeps through the land and leaves
The mountains and valleys bare;
Although the moon reflects brightly on the pond,
The base of the pond remains tranquil.
One may roll jade and use other tactics, laughing out loud, "Ha Ha!"
Gathering right below, it is difficult to recognize one another.

If the true mind cannot be illuminated in this life, then when can the Dharma of seeing the true nature of mind be attained? Only beings that have made the earnest aspiration to become a buddha in their previous lives can establish a connection with the true Dharma in this present life.

You must have thoroughly experienced the realm of great death and been wholly revived back to life in order to freely live the way any great man should live. All practitioners should hold their hwadu and continuously question until what they see, hear, and feel with the discriminating mind is burnt to ashes. Thus, a practitioner will eventually reach the state wherein You will not recognize where you are going, nor will you be aware that you are eating when you take a meal. At that very moment, when you see a form or hear a sound, your mind will be flung wide open.

If the practitioner does not reach this state, then he or she may wander miles and miles away from the ultimate truth of the Buddha. You must therefore transcend any concerns of life and death, ceaselessly investigating your hwadu.

Seon Master Magu came to visit Seon Master Zhangjing, and found him sitting in meditation on his Dharma seat. After circling around Zhangjing three times, Magu raised his Dharma staff, struck it to the floor, and held it there.

Master Zhangjing said, "That is exactly right!"

Right away, Magu went to see Seon Master Nanquan. As he had done with Zhangjing before, Magu circled Nanquan's meditation bench three times and struck the floor with his Dharma staff. In response, Nanguan said, "That is not right, that is not right!"

Upon hearing this, Magu asked Nanquan, "Why do you say that it is not right when Zhangjing confirmed that it was right?"

Master Nanquan replied, "Zhangjing was correct, but you are not correct. That which depends on the power of the wind will eventually be completely destroyed."

After that, Magu departed.

Do you understand the Dharma dialogue between these three Seon masters? This mountain monk will carefully elaborate, point by point.

Magu circled three times around Zhangjing's seat, raised his Dharma staff, and struck it to the floor. Nanquan then said, "That is not right, that is not right!" But Magu inquired, "Why do you say that it is not right when Master Zhangjing said it was right?"

Seon Master Nanquan responded, "Zhangjing was correct, but you are not correct. That which depends on the power of the wind will eventually be completely destroyed."

Therefore, this mountain monk will also circle the meditation seat once and then leave.

The wind that blows over and over has no rest,
The pines and bamboo in front of the mountain stand firmly.

Seen by Neither Sages Nor Animals

September 12, 2011, at Donghwa-sa

> *Those who attain enlightenment can be seen by*
> *neither sages nor guardian generals of the buddhaDharma,*
> *nor by heavenly spirits, ghosts, animals, or birds.*

Heaven and Earth have a single root;
All creations of form and no form are one.
No mind is outside the Dharma,
No Dharma is outside the mind.
A jumble of motley tricks is
All like preaching a dream in a dream.

Everyone, devote this life to bringing light to the truth of the buddhaDharma. There is little guarantee that we shall have another chance to encounter the buddhaDharma in any of our next lives if we fail to attain the truth during this very lifetime.

Everyone should grapple ardently and urgently with a hwadu, or "critical phrase," that spontaneously wells up in one's heart. Keep pursuing the question fervently until only intense doubt remains, and at that very instant, you will crack open the doors to the gate of truth. It is said that it is more likely for a tortoise living in the ocean, rising to the surface only once every three thousand years, to come across a piece of log floating aimlessly in the sea than it is to be born a human fortunate enough to encounter the Dharma teachings. Against such long odds, that miraculous encounter is upon us now. Give everything you have, body and soul, to hold your hwadu at all times, day and night, until it generates a doubt so intense and dense that it bursts forth like a fierce torrent of water, until the whole universe is encased in a mass of doubt. One day, your eyes and ears will open to reality in a single instant, shattering your hwadu and revealing your true self from endless eons ago. In that moment, without moving even a single step, you will reach the pure land and share the full bliss of the buddhas and sages of all ages.

We must walk the correct path to enlightenment by painstakingly following the guidance of an enlightened teacher. That is the only way to repay the kindness and generosity of our patrons; it will liberate us from the cyclical existence of endless births and deaths in the six realms of suffering to revel in the singular joys of nirvana.

Seon Master Taego Bou was a great teacher of the late Goryeo period who secluded himself in a remote hermitage and endured countless hardships and struggles, ferociously striving to achieve enlightenment.

He was given the gongan, "Ten thousands Dharmas return to the one; where does the one return to?" and he investigated this gongan whether he was awake or asleep, sitting or standing. Then, when he happened upon the passage "If everything is gone, nothing moves" in the Sutra of Perfect Enlightenment, his mind suddenly opened wide, and he composed a gatha:

> In perfect stillness,
> A thousand embodiments manifest.
> In restless commotion,
> Not a thing exists.
> What is this that does not exist?
> Chrysanthemums bloom
> After the frost.

Yet he was frustrated by Master Zhaozhou's gongan, "A dog has no buddhanature." He gnawed and gagged on that gongan as if it were a piece of pig iron stuffed in his mouth. He tenaciously applied himself to that gongan, perfectly absorbed only in contemplating it for months on end, even his consciousness lost. Then one day the hwadu was shattered, and he emerged out of samadhi singing a gatha:

> Zhaozhou, the old man,
> Sat and severed the thousand saints.
> A razor-sharp sword of truth was held to the face,
> But not even a hair stirred.

> The fox and the rabbit disappear without a trace;
> Turn the body around, and the lion appears.
> Shattering the adamantine gate,
> Clean and crisp wind blows from time immemorial.

After penetrating that hwadu, he was then confronted by Deshan and Yantou's gongan. It said, "Deshan came out with begging bowls before the bell rang and Yantou whispered secretly into Deshan's ear." But Master Taego Bou persevered unrelentingly and blasted through it, saying:

> Yantou was a superb archer but did not know
> Dew drops can make a flood.
> How many in this world would know the final phrase
> Of supreme truth?

With this thundering exclamation, all gongans were cleanly penetrated and neatly skewered, and all doubts were completely annihilated. Master Bou was 38 years old when the huge chunk of rock lain on his heart for twenty years abruptly disappeared.

Realizing there were no clear-eyed teachers in Goryeo who could test and confirm his enlightenment, Master Bou traveled to Yuan China and wandered around the Chinese continent for one year. He then heard about the glowing reputation of Seon Master Zhu Yuansheng and went to Nanchao, only to find out the master had passed away.

Master Zhu Yuansheng's disciples presented Master Bou with three questions that Master Zhu used to teach them:

First, the aim of renunciant practice is to see one's true nature. Where can one find one's true nature? Second, it is understandable to make a mistake from three thousand miles away, but why can one not see it when it is directly in front of his face? Third (showing two open hands,) this is the secondary phrase. Show me the one phrase of supreme truth.

Master Bou responded:

> I came through the long and winding road to Nanchao looking
> for the old man
>> Who I heard severed the path of ancient buddhas while sitting,
>> Yet roared like a lion.

>> But he reveals neither hand nor foot.
>> Never revealing, but as bright as the sun,
>> Never concealing, but as dark as the blackest lacquer.
>> He returns to parinirvana as I come along;
>> The lingering poison is as bitter as honey.

The disciples were delighted with Seon Master Bou's gatha and implored him to stay, but he turned down their plea, asking them, "I came this far only to meet one person. Where can I find him?" They answered, "Our teachers once said that it is only Shiyu who has achieved the wisdom eye."

Master Bou then walked hundreds of miles and finally had an audience with Seon Master Shiyu Quinggong, the 56th Patriarch and direct Dharma descendent of Master Linji. Master Bou offered three bows and entreated him, "I braved the journey from Goryeo to learn the supreme Dharma from you." Master Shiyu tested him by quoting the story about Master Niutou:

> Once upon a time, when Master Niutou sat in the perfect
> contemplative absorption of samadhi, heavenly pages and maidens
> descended and lavished priceless gifts upon him, and a multitude
> of birds flew in and heaped flowers around him.
> One day, Master Niutou went to his teacher, the Fourth Patriarch

Daoxin, and reported on his progress. Informed of the strange occurrence, Master Daoxin scolded him, "There is no use for the kind of learning that a heavenly throng of spirits and birds could begin to grasp. How dare you claim to know the buddhaDharma with such an incorrect view?"

After that, for Master Niutou there were no more offerings of treasure from heavenly beings or flowers from birds.

Ordinary people may attribute greatness to a person worshipped by heavenly beings and beasts. However, to those who know the truth of the buddhaDharma, such happenings are only cheap parlor tricks worth a few coins. Those who attain the unsurpassed supreme enlightenment of the buddhas and the patriarchs can be seen by neither sages nor guardian generals of the buddhaDharma, nor by heavenly spirits, ghosts, animals, or birds.

After reciting the story, Master Shiyu asked Master Bou, "What do you think of heavenly creatures and birds showering Master Niutou with gifts and flowers?"

"Everyone envies riches."

Shiyu pressed further. "Then what do you think of the fact that the showering of gifts and flowers stopped after Master Niutou spoke to the Fourth Patriarch?"

"In poverty," replied Master Bou, "even sons and daughters stay away."

"Did the empty kalpas during which no Buddha appeared come before time immemorial or after?"

Bou replied, "It abides in time immemorial."

Master Shiyu exclaimed, "BuddhaDharma heads to the East!" He then wrote the epilogue to Master Bou's Poem at Taego Hermitage and conferred his seal of approval. He also designated him as the 57th Patriarch—the 57th direct Dharma descendent of the Buddha himself—by giving Bou his monastic robe, saying, "This robe may belong to my time, but the Dharma abiding in it was passed down from Vulture Peak and exists today in an unbroken lineage. Now I am entrusting you with this truth. Guard it well so that it will flow unceasingly into the future."

Hence, Master Bou received the authentic Dharma of the Buddha. When he returned to Goryeo and lit the lantern of truth, he was exalted to the position of National Teacher by King Gongmin.

The truth of what transpired between Master Bou and Master Shiyu was revealed to the world in its entirety. It conferred a status equal to Bodhidharma on Master Bou and began the lineage of authentic Dharma in Korea that continues to this day. It is due to his beneficence, so lofty as to touch the sky and so spacious as to cover the whole earth, that we now study and practice Seon, the direct path to liberation taught by the Buddha. Therefore, it is important to recognize Master Taego Bou as the forefather of Korea's Seon lineage.

This mountain monk will now render an offering by adding a few words to Seon Master Bou's reply. Please take it to heart.

When asked by Seon Master Shiyu, "What do you think of heavenly creatures and birds showering Master Niutou with gifts and flowers?" Master Bou replied, "Everyone envies riches." This mountain monk would answer:

They come following each other.

Then, to the question of "What do you think of the fact that the showering of gifts and flowers stopped after Master Niutou spoke to the Fourth Patriarch?" this monk would again answer:

They come following each other.

A Perfectly Round Circle

July 4, 2012, at Donghwa-sa

> *If we practice Seon with faith and perseverance,*
> *enlightenment is attainable within three months.*

A mud ox plows the glass earth into nothingness while
A jade horse drinks dry the spring that reflects the bright moon.
Born wearing fur and burdened by horns, arriving as an animal,
How many in the realms of gods and humans understand this truth?

Today this mountain monk would like to tell you about the legacy of Seon Master Gyeongheo.

Master Gyeongheo was the seventy-fifth Patriarch, the legitimate lineage holder of the Dharma of the Buddha's mind seal. He came to this world during the Joseon Dynasty when Buddhism was nearly suppressed into extinction by the followers of Confucianism. He revitalized the tenuous thread of the Seon lineage, then barely surviving in Korea, and brought it back to life, beginning a new era of Seon Buddhism in this land.

Master Gyeongheo joined the monastic order as a very young boy. He studied under the great scholar Master Manhwa Boseon and became highly learned, not only in Buddhist scriptures and treatises but also in a wide range of Confucian and Taoist philosophies and Chinese classics. He was appointed as the chief lecturer of Donghak-sa Temple at the age of 23. Because his knowledge was based on such extensive and in-depth study, his teachings gained subtle yet profound dimensions. Students from all over Korea flocked there to hear him.

One day, he took to the road to meet his old teacher who had first ordained him. He was caught in a heavy rainstorm and forced to take shelter in a small village, where he witnessed the horrible scene of villagers stricken by a cholera epidemic. When he got hungry, he went knocking on doors until a lay Buddhist, a man, welcomed him in and offered him a meal. The villager said, "I once heard that monks accept donations of the four necessities to survive, but if they fail to melt them down, they will be reborn as a cow to pay off their debt." Although Gyeongheo was a scholar of national renown, he suddenly lost all ability to speak and couldn't utter even a single word in reply.

This experience painfully brought home to Master Gyeongheo the futility of Dharma learned through scholarly pursuits in the matters of life and death. He resolved to settle this great issue once and for all. When he returned to Donghak-sa Temple, he asked his students to leave the temple grounds, locking himself in to practice Seon most ardently.

Can anyone now answer on behalf of Master Gyeongheo, a great scholar at that time?

If you correctly see your own true nature, the karma of the past, present, and future will dissipate, and you can be confident even when you encounter tens or thousands of buddhas and generations of patriarchs. No matter what kind of Dharma talk you hear, the correct answer will come to you right away, straight from the depths of your heart like a bolt of lightning. This is the path of seeing one's own true nature.

I offer the one phrase myself:

Yes! I will be the ox,
Becoming the ox, but I eat grass when coming to grass,
And drink water when coming to water.

Master Gyeongheo began his practice by using the teaching of the great enlightened Seon Master Lingyun as his hwadu: "The work of a donkey has not gone yet, but the work of a horse is already arriving." When he encountered this teaching, he faced a "silver mountain and iron wall," a seemingly impenetrable mental block against his progress. He made a hole in the door just big enough to receive one meal per day. Fervently devoted to his practice of hwadu questioning, he stabbed himself in the thigh with an ice pick and placed a sharp knife under his chin to fight off sleep.

After seven years of such arduous practice, he suddenly became singularly focused on his hwadu, totally unaware of seeing or hearing. Three months passed in this manner, fully absorbed in the single-minded samadhi where only the questioning of his hwadu remained. Then one day he heard someone talking outside his door, saying, "Why did you not say that there is no nostril to put the ring through even if one becomes an ox!"

Upon hearing this, he immediately shattered the hwadu, attaining a great awakening and seeing his true nature. Master Gyeongheo then recited this enlightenment verse:

> Hearing that there is no nostril,
> I suddenly realized that the whole universe is my home.
> On the winding roads in June at the foot of Mt. Yeonam,
> Idle farmers leisurely give praise with songs of peace.

Afterward, he received the seal of Dharma transmission from Seon Master Manhwa Boseon. This was in 1879; he was 31.

He attained the cardinal teaching of the unsurpassed supreme truth and revived the nearly extinct Buddha's lineage, succeeding generations of patriarchs. He became perfectly unhindered in giving and taking, in saving life and in taking life; he was fully capable of employing both faculty and function. As such, he caused Ganhwa Seon to flourish once more at a time when the fate of the country hung by a thread.

Thereafter, he devoted the rest of his life to saving sentient beings by performing a wide range of unimpeded actions, completely free from formality or convention, propagating Seon throughout the nation. He also established numerous Seon centers in various locations, arousing in many the aspiration to attain enlightenment. The end result was the eventual appearance of many prominent Seon practitioners and masters.

The teachings of great Seon Master Gyeongheo are the key to the uninterrupted transmission of the Buddha's heart seal up to the present. He fully attained the enlightened spiritual qualities of past Seon masters such as Mazu, Huangbo, and Linji, and proclaimed the Dharma of their Seon lineage throughout the world. In the process, he cultivated many outstanding disciples possessing the wisdom eye, as magnificent as dragons and as ferocious as tigers.

His Dharma heir, Master Hyewol Hyemyeong, and other masters—such as Suwol Eumguan, Mangong Wolmyeon, Chimun Hyeonju, and Hanam Jungwon—were all his direct Dharma descendents and pillars of Korean Buddhism. They played pivotal roles in making the practice of Ganhwa Seon prosper once more throughout the world, the Four Lakes and Five Seas becoming filled with their blessings and beneficence.

Late in life, he opened a small village school on Mt. Gapsan in Hamgyeongdo Province and spent his time teaching children. Then one day, while watching the school children picking weeds, he said, "I feel exhausted," and suddenly lay down. The next day at dawn (April 25, 1912) he picked up a brush and wrote the following parinirvana verse:

> Because the moon of the mind alone is round,
> Its light swallows up the whole universe.
> Having forgotten its light and its boundary altogether,
> What is this thing again?

After completing this verse, Master Gyeongheo added a perfectly round circle. He then set down his brush, lay on his right side and passed into parinirvana. His secular age was 64; his Dharma age 56.

Master Hyewol, the Dharma successor of Master Gyeongheo, belatedly found out about his master's death in the following year, 1913, on July 25, and he and Masters Suwol and Mangong went to Mt. Nandeok in Gapsangun Township to exhume their master's body and cremate his remains according to monastic tradition.

The stench of the decomposing body was unbearable, especially since the body was dug up after a year's time and on a hot summer day. But Master Hyewol, befitting his reputation as the sage who had attained the state of no-mind, personally collected and cremated his master's remains without even the slightest show of discomfort.

Once upon a time, two monks each built huts in adjoining valleys and diligently practiced Seon, living on alms for food. A devoted lay Buddhist, a man, heard a rumor of how dedicated these two monks were in their practice. He took a lump of gold hidden in his closet and went to offer it to them.

He visited one of the monks and said, "I brought you some gold that I own. Please accept it and sell it to purchase medicine, clothing, and any other provisions you may need to help with your practice." But the monk refused to accept it, saying, "I do not have the ability to melt down that gold. Please take it back. Perhaps you could take the gold over to the other side of the mountain, where you will find a monk diligently practicing in another hut."

The man had no choice but to cross the mountain to the other valley and pay his respects to the other monk. He then offered the gold to that monk and said, "I have a small gold nugget passed down through generations in my family. Please accept it and use it to benefit your practice." The monk gladly accepted the gold and responded, "With my great power of practice, I can easily melt down even ten thousand gold pieces."

A few years passed and the first monk, while passing through the village, came across an ox owned by the devout Buddhist who had visited him. He recognized that the ox was in fact the monk who used to practice in the adjoining valley. He had become an ox to pay off the debt of accepting the gold.

The first monk looked at the ox and said, "Now that you are tied up at your old patron's home, are you sure you can successfully melt down that piece of gold again and again?" Upon hearing this, the ox cried out "Mooo—" and lay down, shedding his ox body.

This illustrates the power of how well one can dissolve and resolve matters. Master Gyeongheo practiced rigorously, even placing a sharp knife under his chin to fight off drowsiness. If we practice Seon with such devout faith and perseverance, enlightenment is attainable within three months, and there will appear a second or even third Master Gyeongheo with the ability to expunge all debts and favors.

As illustrated, Seon Master Gyeongheo appeared like a shooting star in the garden of Seon and saved the Seon lineage that was then only hanging by a thread. He was a sage who rekindled the flickering lamp of Dharma once in danger of being extinguished by the winds, founding Seon centers throughout the nation and teaching Seon to many disciples who eventually attained the true "wisdom eye."

Do you understand?

With Great Seon Master Gyeongheo holding up the Dharma staff once,
The darkness of ten thousand years was forever gone,
With one thunderous roar from the master, the whole army of maras and nonbelievers was scattered, shaking in fear, and vanquished.
With every move he made and every step he took, the great Seon Master severed all paths to the six realms of samsara; gone is the suffering of the three planes of the universe.
At times, sitting on the peak of a lofty mountain,
He scolded the Buddha and swore to the patriarchs,
At times, at a crossroad,
Ashes smeared his head, and dust stained his face.

Do you see the original face of Seon Master Gyeongheo?

There are four or five hundred fleshpots lining the streets,
Two or three thousand towers, where people play flutes and zithers.

Hairs Grow out of a Ghost's Fart

May 5, 2012 at Donghwa-sa

If there is even the smallest thought of "I" or the faintest hint of shame,
one cannot do it.

However meticulous, however dignified,
All fall into the secondary and tertiary phrases.
Originally there is not even one thing;
What can possibly be gained again?
If asked, "What is the loftiest Dharma of all the teachings
Delivered over forty-nine years?"
It is the stone man hearing the cry of a wooden rooster at night.

Where was the lineage of the true Dharma, transmitted to Seon Master Gyeongheo, passed? A thread of the mind seal transmitted directly from the Buddha himself is still alive in Korea; it is the thread that Master Gyeongheo, who revived the Seon tradition in Korea, passed on to Master Hyewol, who passed it on to Master Unbong, who passed it on to my teacher, Master Hyanggok, who then passed it on to this mountain monk.

Master Gyeongheo said of his three disciples: "Hyewol's wisdom eye has no equal, the effort and perseverance of Suwol is unsurpassed, and Mangong, due to his good karma, will command a large assembly." Master Hyewol was indeed a great sage highly renowned for attaining the state of no-mind.

Seon Master Hyewol Hyemyeong entered the monastery as a young boy. One day, he sought an audience with Master Gyeongheo and requested, "Please give me a hwadu. I also want to be a sage."

Master Gyeongheo gave him this hwadu: "The body, made of the four elements of earth, water, wind, and fire, is contrived. It cannot teach the Dharma, nor can it listen to the Dharma. Empty space can do neither. However, there is one thing in front of your eyes that is bright and clear and can teach the Dharma. It can listen to the Dharma. So what is this one thing that is bright and clear in front of your face? If you don't know, find this one thing out through questioning and tell me."

Hyemyeong practiced fervently with this hwadu, wrestling with it day and night for seven or eight years, until finally the hwadu became a continuously flowing single-minded thought. One day, Hyemyeong was making straw sandals. In order to make them fit better, he put a shoe into an almost completed sandal and struck it with a hammer. The loud "thwack!" shattered his hwadu.

The young Hyemyeong went straight to see Master Gyeongheo and found him practicing on the wooden veranda. The master noticed Hyemyeong's extraordinary comportment and threw him a question right away, "What is this one thing that is bright and clear in front of your eyes?"

Hyemyeong replied, "Not just me—none of the saints knows it either!"

"What is Hyemyeong then?"

Hyemyeong replied by walking a few steps from east to west, then turned and walked back, stopping right in front of Master Gyeongheo.

"You are right, you are right!" Master Gyeongheo then conferred on him his seal of approval, gave him the new Dharma name Hyewol, and gave his student a Dharma transmission verse. This happened in 1902.

Entrustment to Hyewol Hyemyeong:
If you fully penetrate all Dharmas,
You see the non-beingness in self nature.
Like this, if you awaken to your Dharma-nature,
You will soon see Vairocana Buddha.
Teaching false views by relying on worldly doctrines
Is to carve a blue mountain on the truth that has no letters or

stamp, or to smear glue on the fixed form of the truth.

Then, Master Gyeongheo drew out a chart delineating the lineage of the Dharma lamp transmission and gave it to Hyewol. It was proof that Master Gyeongheo had designated Master Hyewol as his Dharma successor. Master Hyewol spent the rest of his life residing mostly in the south and teaching Dharma to monks at places like Naewon-sa Temple, Tongdo-sa Temple, and Seonam-sa Temple.

Seon Master Hyewol was known for his childlike simplicity and unassuming behavior, free from any false concept of "self" and attachment to things. While he resided at Seonam-sa Temple in Busan, so many practitioners wearing patched robes flocked there that feeding all of them was a struggle. To address this issue, Master Hyewol converted uncultivated land into rice paddies. At one time, the temple sold five parcels of fertile rice paddies and invested the proceeds to cultivate larger tracts of wasteland.

Normally, the money would have been enough to cultivate seven or eight parcels of land after several months of work, but ultimately, only three to four parcels of land were cultivated. What was the reason? It was because whenever hired laborers got tired of working on the land, they would ask Master Hyewol, "Please give us a Dharma talk." Once he began expounding on the Dharma, he would forget the passage of time and go on and on. His students saw this and complained, "If the temple finances are managed in this way, the assembly will all starve to death!"

But the master rebuked them all saying, "You shallow people! The five tracts of good land did not disappear, did they?" He was telling his students that no matter who had the land, as long as it was being farmed, three or four more parcels of arable land were created and given back to the world at the end of the day.

Once you are awakened to the great path, the whole universe is your home. All forms and shapes, in their infinite variety, are not separate from "I." To expand the miniscule world defined by "I" and be liberated is indeed to attain the realm of the sages.

One time, the master accompanied the workers to the market to prepare for the Buddhist funeral rites held during the forty-nine-day period after a person's death. When the master bought a barrel of bean sprouts, all the other venders selling bean sprouts called out to him, "Master, please buy my bean sprouts too!" He wound up buying several barrels, but then had no money left to buy anything else needed for the ceremony.

Another time, Master Hyewol was on his way to the market to make purchases for the final rites of a funeral ceremony. There he saw a woman with her child, weeping and wailing loudly by the roadside. The master inquired what was wrong, and the woman said that she had lost her house in a fire and had nowhere else to stay. He immediately gave her all the money he had, telling her, "Build a new house with this money." He then returned to the temple.

Meanwhile, the monks at the temple were expecting a large amount of goods from the market to be used for the seventh and largest funeral rite, but when no goods arrived, the monks went to see the master. They asked, "Master, it is already late, but for some reason, no goods have been delivered from the market today." Master Hyewol only replied, "The rite has already been performed, and the soul of the departed has gone to the Pure Land."

The next day, when a large number of family and friends of the deceased gathered at the temple and saw no preparations had been made, the head of the family asked what was going on. The master told him about the previous day's encounter and said, "The rite has already been performed, and the soul of the departed has gone to the Pure Land." The family was very happy to hear this and made an additional donation to the temple to purchase a fine offering of food.

As Master Hyewol's fame spread far and wide, the laity competed with each other in offering him fine clothes. When he wore these new clothes, beggars, knowing how little he cared about material possessions approached him and pleaded, "Master, please give us some clothes."

Without hesitation, the master would exchange clothes with them and return to the temple wearing their rags. This kept the laity busy making new clothes for him.

This is in no way an easy act to follow. If there is even the smallest thought of "I" or the faintest hint of shame, one cannot do it. Such acts are like those of a pure, innocent child; the acts of a sage of no-mind. Such acts are rare, even among sages.

One day, dozens of monks were practicing Seon, but they were famished. While the master was away, they took the temple's plow ox, sold it, and with the money had a feast at a restaurant. The master returned and found the ox gone. The next day, after the morning monastic meal, he ordered, "Bring me our ox!"

One of the monks got down on his hands and knees and moved around the room mooing like an ox. Master Hyewol got up and slapped him on the back saying, "This is not the temple ox!" What a marvelous Dharma teaching he blessed the assembly with!

During the Japanese occupation, a newly appointed governor-general named Minami came with a small retinue to have an audience with Master Hyewol; his fame as the sage who had attained the state of no-mind had spread across Korea. After paying proper respect, the governor-general asked him, "Please tell me the most profound and loftiest truth of the Buddha."

Master Hyewol replied: "Buddha's truth? The loftiest and most profound truth? Hairs grow out of a ghost's fart."

Ghosts are already without substance, yet he was saying that these ethereal beings were farting; furthermore, hairs were growing from their farts. What in the world was he talking about? It was something that not only the governor-general couldn't comprehend, but even someone more advanced would have no way of understanding. The governor-general just sat there, unable to say a word, and then left. A rumor that Master Hyewol had hit the governor-general with a club quickly spread, even reaching Japan. One Japanese samurai, a student of Governor-general Minami, heard the story and vowed to himself, "I will go to Korea and teach that Korean monk Hyewol a hard lesson." When he arrived at the master's temple, without even removing his shoes, he barged into the master's room brandishing a long samurai sword. Master Hyewol was sitting on a cushion when the samurai put his naked sword to the master's neck. You must understand that this was a time when the Japanese did not consider Koreans as equals with the same human rights.

However, Master Hyewol maintained his composure and calmly pointed behind the samurai. A guilty conscience needs no accuser. Since he was about to commit the cowardly act of killing an innocent Seon master, he was afraid that somebody was going to attack him from behind. He spun around quickly, and at that moment Master Hyewol jumped up and slapped him on the back shouting, "Take my sword!"

The master's lightning-fast response startled the samurai. In awe of the master's ability, he sheathed his sword and prostrated himself in front of the master, saying, "A great master indeed." Then he left.

In such a dire situation as this, without the penetrating wisdom of a Seon master, one will be unable to wield such a marvelous bejeweled sword at such lightning-quick speed. If Master Hyewol had shown even the slightest fear—had he hesitated even a fraction of a second—he would have lost his head. If one practices correctly and finds the true self, she or he will also be capable of fearlessly wielding wisdom's bejeweled sword.

In the master's later years, he could often be found on the mountain behind the temple, collecting pinecones in a sack. One day, while lifting himself up from a rock where he had stopped to rest, he departed his body in a half-standing posture, the sack full of pine cones still slung over his shoulder. The body of an ordinary being would have fallen to the ground. Ever since the Buddha, countless sages have graced this earth, but hardly anyone has left their body in such a unique posture when they entered paranirvana. Seon Master Hyewol, who perfected the state of no-mind, cast off his physical body in a most unique fashion.

The unhindered freedom that allowed him to pass into parinirvana in this fashion did not come after only one morning of practice. Only after awakening to the path and achieving the boundless samadhi of the true self—after embracing the correct Dharma for a lifetime—is such a feat possible.

If you wish to leave this world in an equally splendid fashion, practice day in and day out, sincerely and ardently focused on your hwadu; focus on it with such single-mindedness that your doubt begins to flow like a river in your everyday life, to the point that you even become unaware of the passage of time.

Do you understand Seon Master Hyewol?

Do not say that no-mind is the path of truth,
No-mind itself is yet another gate obscuring the way.

If You Aspire To Be a Buddha,
The Buddha Is the Mind

October 11, 2011, at Donghwa-sa

Nothing works better than aspiring to be a Buddha.

Although still alive and with sight, it is as good as dead.
Even all medicines are forgotten; how could I be examined by an
Enlightened sage?
Let me tell you this: even the old Buddha has never reached there,
So there is no knowing it. Who can know the scattering of grains of
Sand?

Master Seoku was the teacher who initiated this mountain monk into the
Buddhist monastic order, and one of the greatest Seon masters of this era.
Praised as the "Huineng of Joseon Buddhism" in his time, he was called
the truest Seon adept, the most gracious of all Seon practitioners, and the
greatest of all classical scholars. A truly enlightened master possessing
bright-eyed wisdom and virtue, he presided over many temples, as
dignified as a prime minister over a royal court.

Master Seoku was born in 1875 at Uiryeong, Gyeongsangnam-do
Province, and was considered a prodigy since childhood. With innate
intellect and wisdom, not only did he master all the Chinese classics,

including the texts on Confucian and Taoist philosophies written by famous scholars, but he was also proficient in medical science, poetry, calligraphy, astronomy, and geography.

Before ordination, he lived the life of the "Bodhisattva of Great Compassion" as a healer of the sick and the wounded. Then one day, he was browsing through the Records of Bojo Jinul at Beomeo-sa Temple and found the following verse:

> The three realms are like a burning house, plagued with suffering.
> Why remain and endure?
> If you seek relief from the suffering of cyclical existence,
> Nothing works better than aspiring to be a buddha.
> If you aspire to be a buddha, the Buddha is the mind.

Upon reading this verse, Master Seoku said, "The great path indeed lies within this tradition." He then recited this verse:

> All dust in the field of the mind is gone,
> All clouds cleared from the sky of one's true nature.
> The flowers are smiling and birds are singing in the spring mountains;
> The moon is bright and the wind blows pure in the autumn night.

He then renounced the secular world in search of an enlightened sage. After reaching Jangan-sa Temple on Mt. Geumgang, he had an audience with Seon Master Yeondam Eungsin and joined the monastic order at the age of 38. He received as his hwadu "A cypress tree in the courtyard[6]" from the master, and resolved not to descend from the mountain until he attained great awakening. Master Seoku thus never left the mountain and practiced fiercely at the Mahayeon Seon Center. Inspired by the exemplary perseverance of Master Seoku, three other monks also aroused great

---

6 A monk asked Zhaozhou, "Why did Bodhidharma come from the west?" Zhaozhou replied, "The cypress tree in the courtyard."

courage to seek enlightenment, later becoming three of the most eminent Seon masters of their time, each renowned for his enlightened wisdom eye. They were Masters Mangong, Hanam, and Yongseong.

Master Seoku shattered his hwadu after practicing ardently day and night for twenty years. Upon embracing the ground, he wrote this enlightenment verse:

> Sticking mountains in the ground to build a fence,
> Using the water running through the valley as a cooling fan,
> A passerby reaches such a place and loses all worldly worries.
> It is the idle guest at the lonely hermitage that is rather busy—
> Cleaning the ground and mending clothes, as ragged as drifting clouds.

After attaining enlightenment and seeing his true nature, Master Seoku basked in the eternal and unconditioned bliss of non-action and bellowed a tremendous lion's roar in every direction. He was widely venerated as the "Sage of Mt. Geumgang" by all those in Seon monasteries and the fourfold assembly.

After Korea gained independence from Japan, Seon practitioners initiated a "Buddhist purification movement" in 1954 to rid the Korean Buddhist community of all remnants of the Japanese policy "to obliterate Korean culture," a directive that had been carried out systematically by the Japanese occupation government. After about two years of tireless efforts to reestablish the purity of Korean Buddhism, participants of the purification movement finally formed the Jogye Order of Korean Buddhism, now the representative order of the Korean Buddhist tradition. This was when Master Seoku was elected as the first Supreme Patriarch of the Jogye[7] Order. Although he was not a lineage holder, he was revered by Seon masters and the fourfold assembly alike as the bright-eyed master of all Korean Buddhists.

Seon Master Seoku freely used both "upward and downward" methods to demonstrate enlightenment throughout his lifetime. Then, on his deathbed, he said to his disciples, "This is the end of my connection with

---

7 Jogye (曹溪) is the name of the mountain where the Six Patriarch presided.

these clothes. The end is the freedom from all illusions," and recited this verse of parinirvana:

> The sky and the earth are wrapped in a pouch and tossed outside the world of the ten directions;
> The sun and the moon are picked by a Dharma staff and hidden within a sleeve.
> When the bell stops ringing, the clouds disperse.
> Ten thousand green mountain peaks all become the sunset.

He then sat up straight and, in that position, entered into parinirvana.

On the first anniversary of Master Seoku's death, Master Hyobong, a great admirer of his, ascended the Dharma seat and addressed the assembly:

Seon Master Seoku's Dharma name contains the characters "Boh(普)" and "Hwa(化)." Master Puhua of the Tang Dynasty, who used the same Chinese characters in his Dharma name, spent all his life treading the streets of China while striking his ceremonial hand bell. He then entered into parinirvana by leaving his body behind in a coffin, leaving only the sound of his hand bell floating in the air. Now, how did Bohwa of our time leave us?

One monk stood and roared, "AUUK!"

At this, Master Hyobong said, "That is not correct, not correct!"

So what is the right answer?

Puhua of old left like this, and Bohwa of our time has also left like this.

Do you now understand Seon Master Seoku?

The sound mental faculty of the master is noble and dignified;
The Dharma staff has eyes that distinguish
Even the finest of hair growing in autumn.
Foxes and rabbits are expunged, lifting the spirit of Seon;
Even if they turn themselves into sea dragons,
They will be reduced to ash by lightning.
The sword that gives life and the blade that slays the living,

Flashing like lightning when slashing across the sky,
Ah, indeed a sharp bejeweled sword!

What Are You Expecting By Calling Me?

April 5, 2012, at Donghwa-sa

If you say the path of truth is the path, then that is not the path.

If your mind does not forsake others,
There will be no flicker of shame on your face;
A grandmother's heart is the creed by which this child is cultivated.
A patch-robed monk with the correct wisdom eye will wrest
The teacher's spiritual faculty from him and own it:
Knowing kindness and paying it back,
Deftly and surely manipulating the masterpiece of phrases,
Not affirming when appearing to affirm,
Demonstrating beyond cognitive thinking.

Seon Master Unbong Seongsu became a monk as a young boy and eventually mastered both the sutras and the vinaya; however, he still felt something was lacking. One day, he thought, "I heard there is a path that leads to great enlightenment and the attainment of one's true self. I must become a sage too!" So, Seongsu traveled to see the great southern sage, Seon Master Hyewol. After meeting Master Hyewol, he received his hwadu and practiced diligently for ten years, but his single-minded focus on questioning his hwadu did not "flow purely and unceasingly." So he went to a sacred temple on Mt. Odae where a relic of the Buddha was enshrined. There he prayed ardently for one hundred days with the aspiration, "May my hwadu single-mindedness flow unbroken. May I attain great enlightenment so that the Seon tradition will flourish and all sentient beings may be guided and saved from suffering." He prayed for this every day with all his heart.

After completing one hundred days of prayer, Seongsu went to Unmunam Hermitage at Baekyang-sa Temple for a retreat. After practicing fervently day and night, he finally reached a state where he and his hwadu became one. Early one morning, he opened the door of the Seon room to exit and saw the vast expanse of nature before him—the mountains and brooks beautifully illuminated by the moon. At that moment, he had a great awakening and recited this enlightenment verse:

> Upon opening a door, the cold instantly bites to the bone
> And makes that which formerly gripped my heart suddenly disappear.
> At a dawn when the frosty winds blow, the visitors are all gone.
> The painted pavilion stands alone, and the empty mountain is
> Filled only with the sound of a running stream.

To have his enlightenment confirmed, Seongsu went to Master Hyewol. After paying his respects, Seongsu asked, "I ask about the buddhas of the past, present, and future, and of all the patriarchs. Where do they rest their minds and bodies?"

Master Hyewol just sat quietly. So Seongsu asked again, "Why is it that a living dragon remains immersed in dead water?"

"What would you do?" the master asked back.

In response Seongsu held up a whisk, but the master answered in the negative: "No, it is not!"

"Master," Seongsu then replied, "it has already been a long time since the geese flew by the window."

"I cannot fool you!" the master admitted.

Master Hyewol was satisfied. He entrusted Seongsu with the Dharma lamp of the Linji lineage, gave him the Dharma name Unbong, and bestowed on him a Dharma transmission verse.

All Dharmas that exist and cease to exist
Originally have no true form.
To realize that all phenomena are formless
Is to see their true nature.

Afterward, Master Unbong traveled to Seon monasteries all over the country, instructing monks and assessing their progress. Everywhere he went, he superbly elucidated the profound meaning of Seon. The teaching of the path flourished as never before.

One year at Mangwol-sa Temple, thirty or forty brave monks gathered together and decided to begin a thirty-year long retreat, singularly resolved to attain great awakening. For this retreat, Seon Masters Yongseong and Seoku were appointed "Senior Teacher" and "Elder," respectively. Seon Master Unbong was responsible for maintaining discipline and leading the practice day and night.

One day halfway through the retreat, while giving a Dharma lecture one day, Master Yongseong presented a wonderful Dharma teaching. He asked, "The buddhas of the past, present, and future cannot see my true form. The patriarchs of all ages also fail to see my true form. I ask all of you here now: where can you see this mountain monk?"

When no answer was forthcoming, Master Unbong stood up and said, "A body hidden in a glass jar!"

Master Yongseong, without saying a word, stepped down from the Dharma seat and returned to his quarters.

Today, so that all of you here can cultivate the causes and conditions needed to connect to the path of truth, this mountain monk would like to join in the Seon exchange of these two masters. Listen carefully and take the truth to your heart. Master Yongseong asked, "The buddhas of the past, present, and future cannot see my true form. The patriarchs of all ages also fail to see my true form. I ask all of you here now, where can you see this mountain monk?" Master Unbong responded by saying, "A body hidden in a glass jar!" Master Yongseong then came down from the Dharma seat without saying a word. If this mountain monk were Master Yongseong, I would have said one more thing before descending from the seat:

A true lion bellows a roar truly befitting a lion!

One time, while Master Unbong was in a retreat with Seon Master Mangong's assembly, Mangong gave a Dharma teaching about Seon Master Yunju:

> When Seon Master Yunju finally reentered the world to establish his own sangha, both laity and monastics flocked to join his assembly where he gave a teaching every month. However, there was one hermit who had lived for several decades in a small hut on the same mountain. He never showed up even once to listen to the Dharma talks or pay respect to the newly installed senior teacher. One day, Master Yunju told his attendant to go see the hermit.
>
> The attendant arrived at the hermitage and asked, "The new senior teacher gives Dharma talks at the temple. Why do you not come down to listen?" The hermit responded, "Even if Shakyamuni Buddha himself blessed us with his presence, I still would not enjoy listening to his teaching."
>
> When the attendant told the master about what happened, the master ordered the attendant to deliver a set of fine summer clothing as a gift to the hermit.
>
> When the attendant presented the clothing to the hermit, he refused it, saying, "The clothes I inherited from my parents would last me for all my life and even longer. Why would I accept these? Take them back!"
>
> When the attendant brought the clothes back and reported to the master, Master Yunju gave him one more errand, and the attendant set out once again up the mountain. "Sir," the attendant asked the hermit, "what clothes did you wear before you were born?"
>
> The hermit could not respond appropriately. A few days later, the hermit passed away in a sitting posture. All the monks on the mountain got together and prepared for his cremation ceremony. When they finally set fire to the funeral pyre, five colors of radiant light shot through the sky and numerous relics were found in the ashes. The whole mountain was abuzz with the story of this

mysterious happening.

When Master Yunju heard of this, he placed the variegated relics in his palm and said, "Even though you discarded your body in a sitting position and your relics shine brightly in fabulous colors, it is still nothing compared to a correct answer to my question."

At that, the relics and the dazzling rainbows in the sky all suddenly disappeared.

Seon Master Mangong then asked the assembly this question about this Dharma teaching: "If that hermit had the correct wisdom eye open to truth, why would he not answer the question? If he did not have the correct wisdom eye open to truth, how is it that he was able to give up his body while sitting, leaving behind multi-colored relics and generating beautiful light?"

When no one replied, Master Unbong stood up and offered this magnificent answer: "In the summer, wear exquisite linen made in Andong; in winter, wear fine cotton produced in Jinju."

In his later years, after having traveled extensively and taught at Seon monasteries all over the country, Master Unbong established his residence at Myogwaneum-sa Temple near Busan. One month before his death, his disciple, Master Hyanggok, asked him, "Master, when are you going to leave this world and enter parinirvana?"

"On the day when the tail falls off of the rabbit," Master Unbong answered without hesitation.

The second month in the lunar calendar is the month of the rabbit, and the last day is the tail. On the last day of the month, the master assembled his disciples and said, "I will enter parinirvana today. If any of you have doubts, ask now."

Master Hyanggok asked, "What is the path of Buddha's truth?"

"If you say the path of truth is the path, then that is not the path."

Master Hyanggok then asked, "Where is the road to nirvana?"

"Ouch! Ouch!"

"After you pass away, who shall we rely on to guide us in practice?"

Master Unbong started tapping and singing to the rhythm of a folksong:

Yo~ho yo~ho yo~horo sangsa di ya

All of you farmers don't despair over there being no rain.
Rain is brushing by the peak of Mt. Galbi over there.
Wrap your rain clothes around your waist
And put on your bamboo hat.
Let's go out to the fields and pick the weeds!
Ollol lollollol sangsa di ya! duridung, duridung

When he was finished, he lay down to die, but his attendants cried out, "Master, Master!" The master asked, "What are you expecting by calling me?" then entered parinirvana.

Master Unbong's teacher, Seon Master Hyewol, departed his body with a sack of pine cones slung over his shoulder in a half-standing posture; Master Unbong shed his body after transmitting Dharma to his disciple on the day the "rabbit's tail falls off." These are indeed spectacular ways to enter parinirvana.

Do you understand Master Unbong's meaning?

He clearly is endowed with the wisdom eye of truth to be the teacher of both gods and humans.

Suddenly Seeing Two Hands

March 7, 2012, at Donghwa-sa

If you attain Hyanggok's five samadhis, you will be unhindered everywhere.

**This mountain monk has just shown this Dharma staff
To the assembly.
Even if this truth was understood before the staff was held up,
It is still far away.
But if this truth was understood after this staff was held up,
It is even more distant, 108,000 miles afar.
Even if this truth was understood before the staff was held up,
Everyone in this assembly heads east,
But this mountain monk heads west.
Take the profound meaning of this question to heart:
Why did I say that even if this truth was understood
Before the staff was held up, everyone in this assembly heads east,
But this mountain monk heads west?
The red fog pierces to the bottom of the blue ocean,
The bright sun and Mt. Sumeru wrap around each other.**

The four continents make up a universe. They are located to the south, east, west, and north of Mt. Sumeru, which stands at the center. The world of samsara—our world—is on the southern continent of Jambudvipa. The sun is always revolving around Mt. Sumeru.

One day, my teacher, Seon Master Hyanggok Hyerim (1912-1978), went with his mother to visit his older brother, a monk at Naewon-sa Temple on Mt. Cheonseong. Deeply inspired after seeing dozens of monks solemnly practicing, the future master told his mother: "I must become a monk like my brother and an enlightened sage. Please return home without me." He joined the monastic order right then. He was sixteen years old.

Receiving a hwadu from Master Unbong, the senior teacher of Naewon-sa Temple, he wrestled with his hwadu for two years while working in the temple kitchen. Once the meal was served, he would clean the kitchen and sit on the floor to investigate, questioning his hwadu ardently, day after day. One spring day, he was concentrating on his practice after work while the doors to his room were open. Suddenly, the wind blowing from the valley slammed the doors shut. The moment he heard the doors slam shut with a loud BANG, his hwadu shattered.

At that time, he was just an acolyte, still not formally initiated into the Buddhist order. However, he immediately went to see Master Unbong. When the master saw this young kid walking confidently into the room, his head still unshaven, the master knew the young acolyte was special. The master pushed toward him the wooden pillow lying by his side and said, "Speak! Speak!" The acolyte immediately kicked the wooden pillow away.

How dare an eighteen-year-old acolyte kick away a wooden pillow in the presence of a great master? It was simply unacceptable behavior to an elder, but Master Unbong kept urging him to answer: "Not correct! Speak again!" The acolyte answered, "Thousands and tens of thousands of words are nothing but nocturnal ramblings! The buddhas and sages of all ages have deceived me."

How could a mere acolyte, not yet ordained, burst out with such words without hesitation? Once one sees one's true nature, he sees the home of the mind, the origin itself. That is how one is able to answer right away as the young man did.

Later, this acolyte was ordained under the name Hyerim and received the novice precepts from Master Unbong. Hyerim received special care and guidance for the next ten years, until 1941 when Master Unbong gave him a new Dharma name, Hyanggok, and bestowed on him a Dharma transmission verse just before passing away.

> *Entrustment to my Dharma successor, Hyanggok Hyerim:*
> Truth from the west that has no letters or stamp
> Cannot be given or taken.
> If liberated even from that which cannot be given or taken,
> The crow flies, and the rabbit runs.

Later, in 1947, realizing how greatly weakened and suppressed Seon practice had been under thirty-five years of Japanese rule, Master Hyanggok and his Dharma friends decided to begin an intense three-year retreat to revive the spiritual foundation of Korean Ganhwa Seon. At Bongam-sa Temple, twenty monks from all over the country, including Seongcheol, Cheongdam, and Wolsan, made a determined vow that, even if it cost them their lives, they would, "put aside what we have known before. Completely renew our practice, and devote ourselves fully so as to attain great enlightenment."

One hot summer day, as Hyanggok, Seongcheol, and Cheongdam were sitting on a wooden veranda practicing in the stifling heat, Master Seongcheol asked a question, quoting the Dharma teaching of an old master: "A sage of the past says, 'You must kill a dead man completely to see the living, and revive a dead man completely to see the dead.' Cheongdam, do you understand the meaning of this?"

Master Cheongdam stammered, not knowing what to say. Master Hyanggok, who was next to him, could not answer either. This aroused in Master Hyanggok a great resolve. He wrestled with this hwadu so fervently that he entered a state of samadhi while leaning against the balustrade of a pagoda. He was no longer aware of the sweat trickling down his body in the oppressive heat, or of the heavy rain soaking his robe. Greatly inspired by this, the assembly said, "Look at Master Hyanggok! He is so deep in samadhi that he doesn't even know it is raining!" Fiery resolve and great joy were kindled in their minds, and they all put even more effort into their practice.

For twenty-one days, Master Hyanggok remained totally absorbed in single-minded focus on this hwadu. All boundaries fell away; he was unaware of seeing or hearing, even losing awareness of his own body.

Then, one day while walking around the temple grounds, completely deaf and dumb, he suddenly had a great awakening when he saw his two hands swinging as he walked. He then sang this enlightenment verse:

Suddenly seeing two hands, the whole is revealed.
All buddhas of the past, present, and future are
Nothing but puppets in the eyes.
Thousands of scriptures and ten thousand theories,
What kind of a thing are they?
Because of this, all buddhas and patriarchs lost their bodies.
One laugh at Bongam-sa Temple in eternal happiness;
Idyllic are the winding folds of Mt. Hiyang over 10,000 kalpas.
The bright wheel of the moon will come again next year,
The crane cries anew where the golden autumn wind blows.

Master Hyanggok's awakening at that moment was of great significance. Although a few Korean Seon masters, such as Taego Bou and Hwanam Honsu, had received direct transmission of the Dharma from a Chinese master, and therefore possessed the true "wisdom eye," the true Seon teaching had not been properly passed down to succeeding generations, and the true wisdom eye open to the highest truth had been lost. However, through Master Hyanggok's awakening, the path to supreme truth was restored and the Buddha's most fundamental Dharma revived.

Master Hyanggok immediately called in Master Seongcheol and asked him, "A sage of the past says, 'You must kill a dead man completely to see the living, and revive a dead man completely to see the dead.' Do you understand the meaning of this?" But Master Seongcheol himself could not answer and hesitated. The two of them were both born in 1912 and, since their twenties, had been very close. Nevertheless, when no answer was forthcoming, Master Hyanggok rebuked Master Seongcheol loudly and asked him again by quoting another Dharma teaching:

During the Tang Dynasty, there was a great master named Weishan who taught an assembly of 1,500 monks. Every morning, his two disciples, Yangshan and Xiangyan, came to pay their respects to Master Weishan, the senior teacher of the temple. One day, the two disciples came in the morning to greet their master, but Master Weishan stayed lying in bed.

Yangshan came in, bowed three times, and greeted him: "Master, did you sleep well last night?" Master Weishan turned over in bed to face the wall and said, "I had a dream last night. Interpret the dream for me." As soon as Yangshan heard this, he went outside, brought in a washbasin full of water, put it beside Master Weishan, and left the room.

Xiangyan came in next and asked after the master's health, "Master, did you sleep well last night?" Master Weishan rolled over again on the bed and replied, "I had a dream last night. Interpret the dream for me." Xiangyan immediately went outside, brewed tea with utmost care, and brought it back to the master. Delighted, Master Weishan praised them highly, "The wisdom and supernormal capabilities of my two disciples are better than those of Sariputra and Maudgalyayana at the time of the Buddha."

Master Hyanggok again asked Master Seongcheol the meaning of this Dharma exchange, but he was hesitant and could not answer. "You're just wasting the temple's food," said Master Hyanggok. He then grabbed Master Seongcheol by the collar, pushed him out of the temple and locked the gate. "Until you respond correctly to this Dharma teaching, you cannot reenter this gate!" How marvelous! What great practitioners they were!

It is difficult to be that firm to one's close friend. Furthermore, what an excellent attitude Master Seongcheol displayed! He proved himself to be more than worthy of seeing his true nature by fully embracing such harsh words from a close friend.

Seongcheol, then 36, was now locked out of the temple by his close Dharma friend, Master Hyanggok, and could not return to the temple. So he stayed outside and practiced fiercely on the dialogue day and night, fueled by great resolve. After pouring his heart and soul into practice for days, even forgoing food, he finally attained a great enlightenment. Master Seongcheol immediately ran to the temple in the middle of the night and pounded on the gate with a big rock.

That was a time when there were many communist guerrillas in the mountains. When this loud banging sound reverberated over the mountain in the middle of the night, the people in the temple were fearful. They thought the guerrillas had come down from the mountains. However, Master Hyanggok knew who was making the racket. He went to the gate and shouted, "Speak! If you answer correctly, I'll open this gate!"

Master Seongcheol immediately responded correctly, and Master Hyanggok opened the gate. They hugged and danced with joy for some time. What a magnificent and beautiful sight it must have been! Master Hyanggok had practiced ardently and attained a great awakening because of Master Seongcheol, and Master Seongcheol had practiced ardently and attained a great awakening because of Master Hyanggok, who had kicked him out of the temple.

Their great awakening opened wide the world of truth—it was a huge leap in the history of Korean Seon Buddhism at a time when the wisdom eye that sees truth was sorely lacking. This mountain monk bows my head low to them with utmost respect.

Master Hyanggok was not fooled by the gongans of the world's great patriarchs. He gave Dharma teachings like a lion's roar, boundless and without hesitation. After he attained awakening at Bongam-sa Temple, he met with many bright-eyed masters and spread the Dharma of supreme truth far and wide. In the process, the world came to know that his enlightenment was directly transmitted from the loftiest truth of the Buddha and the patriarchs, and that he had opened a new chapter on supreme truth in Korea's Seon tradition. As such, he was invited to serve as senior teacher at many Seon monasteries and instruct many practitioners. Later, he opened a Seon center at Myogwaneum-sa Temple on Korea's southeast coast near Wollae, where he lived the life of a great master, ushering in a new and flourishing era of Seon Buddhism.

In autumn of the year when this mountain monk turned 30, Master Hyanggok took me as his attendant to Mangwol-sa Temple in Gyeonggi Province, where Master Chunseong had presided for a long time. Sitting on a wooden bench, Master Chunseong welcomed Master Hyanggok, and they discussed Dharma. Master Chunseong told Master Hyanggok the following as they drank tea:

"For the three months of our last retreat, I served nice meals to the assembly under the guidance of the senior teacher, but on the morning of the last day, I decided to collect the dues for the meals. When the morning meal was finished and before the assembly stood up, I said to the assembly, "Allow me to speak." Then I continued, "When I went up behind the Mountain God Shrine yesterday evening, I met a blue lion. I ask all of you, what would you do?" The senior teacher said, "I would say, 'Attendant, come out and bow one time.'" If the attendant had bowed, he would have been devoured. I am afraid that the dues I collected were unsatisfactory."

Master Chunseong then asked Master Hyanggok, "What would you do if it were you?" Before the question even ended, Master Hyanggok made the sound of a lion, "Raaaawr!" Master Chunseong heard Master Hyanggok's roar and marveled, saying, "You are indeed the enlightened master of the South."

Thereafter, Master Hyanggok came down to Myogwaneum-sa Temple to stay. One day, he mounted the Dharma seat and expounded on the five kinds of samadhi:

> The first samadhi involves grasping time and space tightly and stabilizing them so as not to let even the tiniest thing escape, to not let even a single tongue enter. This is the "immovable samadhi" of a monk in a patched robe.
>
> The second samadhi involves emitting light from the crown of the head and illuminating the whole world in the four directions; it is also to embrace all things one by one. This is the "diamond eye" of a monk in a patched robe.
>
> The third samadhi involves making gold by transforming iron and making iron by transforming gold, grabbing it suddenly, and releasing it suddenly. This is the "Dharma staff" of a monk in a patched robe.
>
> The fourth samadhi involves making people hold their tongues, not even letting them breathe, and then driving them backward, tumbling and rolling, 3,000 miles away. This is the "spirit" of a monk in a patched robe.
>
> The fifth samadhi involves not even blinking your eyes or turning your face to see, even if all the buddhas of the ten direction, all the buddhas of the past, present, and future, Manjushri and Samantabhadra, and the world's greatest bright-eyed masters

all appeared together, radiated great light, and saved countless sentient beings. This is the "special state of embracing" of a monk in a patched robe.

If all of you clearly attain Master Hyanggok's five samadhis one by one, you will be unhindered everywhere and not fooled by others' deceptions.

Another day, Master Hyanggok ascended the Dharma seat and gave this unsurpassed teaching:

> Even if you rain down blows with the staff and shout roars that roll like thunder, you have not even come close to the supreme truth of Seon. Even if one knows the buddhas of past, present, and future, he cannot share. Even the patriarchs cannot reveal it in its entirety. One is still unable to write proper commentaries on it, even if the entire collection of scriptures is at his fingertips. Even bright-eyed monks in patched robes have no solution. Furthermore, using any word, even the single character for Buddha is still to be swayed by human intentions and emotions; the character for Seon itself is a mass of shame.
>
> Even if all the buddhas of the past, present, and future, Manjushri and Samantabhadra, the world's greatest bright-eyed masters, and millions of saints expounded the Dharma again and again until all future time was exhausted, not only would it fail to get you closer even by the breadth of a hair but you would regress by 10,000 miles.
>
> If you speak or write about it, it recedes even farther. Therefore, if you wish to attain Dharma, you must elucidate the fundamental source that lies beyond words and letters and illuminate the cardinal teaching that is beyond any spiritual faculty.
>
> Even if one is already within it, if even the slightest thought of Buddha or Dharma penetrates, even less than the tip of a hair, the arrow has already disappeared into the western sky. What should you do then?

It is no use even if you cry until you shed tears of blood.
It is better to spend the rest of the spring with your mouth shut.

In this style, Master Hyanggok proclaimed the Dharma of the Buddha's heart seal throughout his life. When he was nearing death, the master came to stay at Haeunjeong-sa Temple. Three days before he entered parinirvana, he called this mountain monk and left this verse:

> A man made of stone plays a flute on a mountain peak
> While a woman made of wood dances happily along the stream.
> If one takes one more step into time, even back before
> The age of the King Buddha of the Majestic Voice[8],
> His world of truth will be always bright; he can always reap and
> Use it.

With that, Seon Master Hyanggok entered parinirvana.

The master, who had proclaimed the wondrous teaching of Seon for so long, once asked me a question by quoting the following story:

> After Master Mangong entered parinirvana at Sudeok-sa Temple, Master Yongeum served as the senior teacher for five retreats. Later, after the position was left unoccupied for several years, Master Gobong became the new senior teacher. One day, as he was about to ascend the Dharma seat to give a talk, Master Geumo grabbed the hem of Gobong's robe and said, "Please say something before you mount the Dharma seat."
>
> When someone asks you to say something before ascending to the Dharma seat, the right thing to do would be to respond immediately. But, Master Gobong only said, "Let go of my robe!"
>
> Geumo asked him again, "Please say something before ascending the Dharma Seat."
>
> "Let go of my robe!"
>
> The exchange continued like this for a while, one grabbing the robe and the other yanking it back.

Forty years later, Master Hyanggok asked this mountain monk, "If you were Master Gobong, what would you have said?" This mountain monk

8 威音王佛: A buddha who lived in the extremely distant past.

bellowed a thunderous "AUUK!" Master Hyanggok examined my response and said, "If you roar like that it will blind all the people in Busan."

"It is this humble monk's fault," I said.

He replied, "It is this old monk's fault."

Do you understand this exchange?

If you wish to attain truth of Master Hyanggok and this mountain monk, you must perceive this Dharma teaching correctly. Only then will you correctly perceive and attain the truth passed down through Master Hyanggok's lineage.

World Peace through Ganhwa Seon

September 15, 2011, at Riverside Church, New York City

> *Awakening to true self is hope for the human race;*
> *from here, the future will open up.*

Mind, mind, mind!
So difficult to find.
Try, but you'll never see it.
Just sit in no-mind,
Mind sits right there too.

Ladies and gentlemen, look, look!

As I begin, I would first like to express my gratitude and delight to all of you who have taken time out to be in attendance here tonight at Riverside Church. I am aware that many different religious leaders have come also. This mountain monk has come to this sacred site not to compare different religious traditions and talk about which one is superior, but to introduce you to the spiritual culture of Asia as one step in the process of fostering world peace.

Not limiting ourselves by ideology or religious doctrine, soon we will be able to communicate directly, mind to mind. All religions should act as siblings and good neighbors, helping each other to find inner peace and

Mind, mind, mind!
So difficult to find.
Try, but you'll never see it.
Just sit in no-mind,
Mind sits right there too.

making the world a better place.

Tonight, this mountain monk would like to introduce "questioning meditation," what we Koreans call Ganhwa Seon. This is the heart of our spiritual culture in Asia. Ganhwa Seon is a superb practice that transcends religion and ideology. It will create understanding and generate world peace as well as guide us to awakening. When you awaken to your true self and arrive at the mind's home, then, like a child in his or her mother's arms, all kinds of arguments disappear. There is no conflict, jealousy, or envy here; you will be able to enjoy peace and freedom while displaying great wisdom.

Awakening to true self means to awaken to the master within. I ask each one of you, what is sitting here listening to me speak right now? When you awaken to this master within, it will become the master everywhere, living a free life without hindrance. By not relying on anything but this unchangeable true self, you will be liberated from all religious, political, and cultural restraints and live harmoniously with all beings. Awakening to true self is hope for the human race; from here, the future will open up.

So how can we awaken to true self and arrive at the home of the mind? How can we enjoy peace forever?

The most important thing is to first meet an authentic, clear-eyed teacher who has awakened to true self. The mind's true home is so vast and boundless, profound and recondite, it is impossible to arrive there through one's own power alone. You must meet a clear-eyed teacher and firmly make a vow that you will attain great awakening and see your own true nature. Question the following topic, or hwadu, without ever forgetting it:

What is my true self from before I was born?

This inquiry is what we call Ganhwa Seon. By constantly maintaining single-minded concentration through Ganhwa Seon, you will arrive at the mind's home; wisdom shining like the sun and the moon will radiate from you while you simultaneously attain great compassion and love. In this state, you will become one body with the whole human race, one household with all sentient and insentient beings. This is how we will be able to bring great peace to the world.

As an ancient sage said, "People live in poverty because of lack of wisdom." If people want to be successful, enjoy good fortune and receive blessings in their life, then they must arrive at the mind's home and attain the eye of marvelous wisdom.

How do we practice in order to awaken to true self?

The easiest way to practice Seon is by sitting in meditation, so you must learn how to do this correctly. Sit comfortably on your mat in the morning and evening. Straighten your back, expand your chest, and place both hands on your lap below your belly button. This is called your *danjeon*. Look six feet in front of you and focus your concentration on your topic of inquiry, the hwadu, at that spot. Concentrate with your eyes open so that you don't succumb to drowsiness or distracting thoughts. While continuing to sit, extend your practice to fill every moment.

Whether you're coming or going, sitting or standing, working or sleeping, you earnestly focus on questioning your hwadu without ever forgetting it. In this way, keep pushing forward again and again, raising the question about the hwadu: "What is my true self from before I was born?" Continue to bring it up tens of thousands of times without ever forgetting it; there will be no space for any distraction to arise. To give you an example, it is like a mortar in a water mill—if the water wheel is not turning, the mortar will not pound the grain, but once the wheel starts turning, the mortar will pound all day long. In the same way, I tell you to keep pushing forward with the question tens of thousands of times because once you become trained in this kind of questioning, all of a sudden you will reach a new point in your practice: true questioning. The questioning of the hwadu will not cease for even a moment, but will flow continuously. This single-minded questioning will keep flowing along day and night just like a running stream. When you are sitting in Seon, you will be unaware whether it is day or night; you will forget everything you see and hear. In this way, you become completely absorbed in the single-minded questioning of hwadu. As time passes, there will ultimately be an instant when, upon seeing an object or hearing a sound, your hwadu will unexpectedly shatter.

At that point, the eye of wisdom naturally opens and will remain forever brilliant. You will then guide all people to the truth. As a great teacher in both Heaven and Earth, you will be completely free and unhindered. In this way, when you reach the mind's home without taking a single step, you will enjoy glorious freedom and happiness. You will truly contribute to peace for all humankind.

In true self, there is immutable integrity. In true self, there is eternal happiness. In true self, there is great freedom that is devoid of all hindrances. In true self, there is true peace that comes from complete impartiality. Such integrity, happiness, freedom, and impartiality cannot be obtained merely through education or wealth, how devoutly you live your life, or through your position or sterling reputation. Rather, only a person who has awakened to true self can be so blessed.

Even if in this lifetime you do not attain the state of single-minded samadhi on the hwadu, if you were to practice Ganhwa Seon continuously throughout your everyday lives, then all discrimination, disputes, and conflicts would disappear and your minds would naturally be at repose. At the moment of death, with a clear mind and bright spirit, you will let go of this physical body, just as if you were changing clothes; and in the next life you will definitely attain great awakening.

However, if you neglect Seon practice, you will waste your life in discrimination, disputes, and conflicts. The result will just be suffering and entanglements. On your deathbed, it will be too late to have regrets about how you wasted your life.

Thus, I hope all of you will continuously cultivate this practice of Ganhwa Seon, or questioning meditation, so that you will learn to hold the hwadu even when you are singing a lullaby to a crying baby. By living this way, you'll have a commendable family and your household will live in perfect concord. If everyone practices like this, then our society and country will also be in perfect harmony; this will become a driving force in forging world peace.

About a hundred years ago, there was an enlightened Seon master in Korea named Mangong (1871-1946). One day, as he was sitting on the veranda chatting with several of his disciples, a bird took off from the eaves. Master Mangong asked, "How many miles will that bird fly in a day? If any of you have an answer, let's hear it." A little later, Master Bowol stood up and gave this truly wonderful response: "The bird hasn't traveled even a couple of steps." What a splendid exchange of truth this was!

One day, thirty or forty dedicated monks from all over Korea gathered at Mangwol-sa Monastery. They were determined to see their true natures and have a great awakening, so they forbade themselves from leaving the monastery and entered into a period of fierce meditation. They appointed Yongseong Sunim (1846-1940) to be the resident Seon master; Seoku Sunim (1875-1958), who would later become the first head of the Jogye Order, was the senior Seon practitioner; and Unbong Sunim (1889-1944) acted as the leader of the meditation hall. When they were halfway through the ninety-day retreat period, Master Yongseong climbed up on the high seat and challenged them with this splendid question: "My true appearance cannot be seen by any of the sages of past, present, or future, or by enlightened masters of all generations. Those of you in the assembly here today: where can you see this mountain monk's true appearance?"

Unbong Sunim then stood up and gave this definitive answer: "You've hidden your body inside a glass jar."

Without responding, Master Yongseong immediately descended from the high seat and returned to his residence. Ladies and gentlemen in attendance here at Riverside Church, how would you answer if you were asked, "My true appearance cannot be seen by any of the sages of past, present, or future, or by enlightened masters over many generations. Where can you see this mountain monk's true appearance?" If any of you can give me an answer, let's hear it.

Attendant! Lock the door!

Do you understand?

Originally there is no birth or death. The four elements—earth, water, fire, and wind—fundamentally do not exist. Both the five elements and the spiritual world are actually empty. I hope you understand these truths through my Dharma talk. Let go of all of your attachment, hate, and resentment, and rest in peace forever.

What do you think?

As the clouds lift from the mountaintop, the ridgeline appears —
Only the bright moon floats atop the waves in the sea.

What is your true self?

Thank you very much.

At the National Prayer Breakfast

February 2, 2012 at the National Prayer Breakfast International Luncheon hosted by U.S. Congress in Washington D.C. .

Jesus was very close to the Buddhist bodhisattva ideal.

As the leader of twenty thousand monks and twenty million laypeople in Korea, it is my honor to be invited here to bring to all of you, distinguished leaders from around the world, greetings and blessings of peace.

I am grateful that great masters from the Council of Elders have chosen me as the leader to represent the Jogye Order; I will follow the definitive opinions from the Council of Elders to create a peaceful future. I will do my utmost to propagate Ganhwa Seon, the essence of oriental spiritual culture, throughout the world.

The Buddha gave great blessings to the world and established the ideal of enlightenment, of Buddhahood, which many individuals embodied throughout the centuries. Since today, here, at this important gathering, many leaders are speaking about the significance of Jesus in their religious traditions, I want to add my own reflections.

Jesus, in his teachings, was very close to the Buddhist bodhisattva ideal. Jesus embodied a supreme form of a bodhisattva's mercy through his teaching of nonviolence, compassion, and peace, being a servant instead of a master. His understanding that one can gain the whole world and still lose one's own soul made him an ideal object of devotion for the world.

There is a profound potential for mutual enrichment through dialogue among all the great religions of the world, not merely in the field of ethics and spirituality—which embody compassion, love, meditation, and the enhancement of tolerance—but also in the practice of charity and helping the poor, eliminating ignorance and leading towards understanding, and eradicating hunger and disease. I feel that this dialogue could go very far.

Spring comes—for whom do the flowers bloom?
In the place a partridge cries,
The fragrance of a hundred flowers fills the air.

The Whole World is Under One Roof
Dharma Talk at the Installation Ceremony of the Supreme Patriarch

March 28, 2012, at Jogye-sa

Be with people in need and people in pain.
Love and cherish the impoverished and the sick
as you would take care of your own body.

Trampling and penetrating the foreheads of a thousand saints,
The mundane and the supra-mundane cannot discern it by thinking.
If you can fully attain the unborn truth underneath this staff,
With one leap, you join the ranks of all buddhas.
The nirvana of perfect stillness and non-being is benevolent,
righteous, gracious, wise;
Benevolent, righteous, gracious, and wise is the nirvana of perfect
stillness and non-being.
Embracing the path of supreme truth,
The wind blows, the grass bows down.

It is said, "People live in poverty because they lack wisdom; the horse grows feeble and its hair gets long." Everybody wishes to enjoy good fortune and great success lifetime after lifetime. If so, consider this hwadu, whether awake or asleep, over and over again, until your single-minded focus on it flows unceasingly:

What is my true self from before I was born?

In one's true self lies luminous wisdom; in one's true self lies great fortune; in one's true self lies great compassion; in one's true self lies perfect peace and magnificent freedom. If you attain your true self and reach the home of the mind, you will have an unimpeded command of the splendid exhibition of truth, furled and unfurled at will. If you cannot awaken to your true self in this lifetime, how can you ever hope to conquer life and death at all?

Seon is the quickest way to overcome the mind's myriad conflicting and distracting thoughts; it is the supreme shortcut to finding truth. Practice sincerely and diligently in your daily life, and you will cultivate wisdom and peace of mind and become a teacher of truth both in Heaven and on Earth.

Even a million gold coins are not enough if people fight over them; Even a few coins will not be used up if people decline them.

Brothers and sisters of the Four Lakes and Five Seas! The mountains provide fresh air and nurture all kinds of animals and birds. Water nourishes all sorts of fish and shellfish while blessing both sentient and non-sentient beings with life. You should all practice the virtues exemplified by the mountains and the waters of the earth.

The whole world is under one roof; "others" and "I" are not two in our countless manifestations.

Be with people in need and people in pain. Love and cherish the impoverished and the sick as you would take care of your own body.

What do you think of this final word of truth?

Where can you find this thing that shines for ten thousand years to come?
Every form and every shape reveals this truth of old.

World Peace and the Ecological Crisis:
Buddhist Wisdom

October 4, 2012, at the United Nations-sponsored World Religious Leaders Meeting held at the UN Plaza in New York City.

> *The whole world is just one;*
> *things are not separate from me,*
> *nor are they separate from you.*

As religious leaders, our raison d'etre, our responsibility and duty, is to help those suffering and heal the world's ills. We are not truly religious if we do not address these issues. Without the belief and trust of neighbors, who are suffering in anxiety and pain, religious leaders cannot be true to their calling.

We religious leaders must awaken people and show them a model. We must give first, we must reach out our hands first, we must take care of others first in order to relieve hunger and sickness. We must awaken people to cease their fighting and hatred and recover the environment and the ecosystem.

I deeply believe that this is the reason that all religions exist. In order to fulfill these duties, this mountain monk will try to teach Ganhwa Seon practice while also starting to work with relief organizations and environmental groups.

We have not been good caretakers to the earth. The global changes observed in the last two hundred years are far greater than those that have occurred over the previous thousands of years. We do not know whether our planet or mankind can survive this new crisis or not. We almost forget that this earth, this nature has been handed down to us from our ancestors, with their special wish for us to keep it healthy and clean.

We must realize how interconnected we are with the earth and one another—with the earth that houses us and with the human beings that make up our communities. Consider, where do we as individuals begin and end? Where do our lungs end and the air we breathe begin? How can we walk without the ground beneath our feet? I join you with my lifelong wish to work harder for the coming generations. Now, some of these changes, these challenges, are extremely detrimental and may even be irreversible. But in these challenges are great opportunities as well.

By practicing Ganhwa Seon, which is a way to transcend the false self, we discover the way to the true self. This is what must be taught—a way of meditation that uncovers the true self and provides a proper preparation and orientation for action.

"How can Buddhist teachings of Ganhwa Seon meditation help?" you may ask. Buddhist teaching is ancient, going back more than 2,500 years and contributing to human spiritual and cultural development. Korean Buddhism, since its inception 1,600 years ago, has followed the authentic Dharma lineage; it aims at establishing eternal world peace through a new paradigm, a fresh direction for our materialistic culture. This mountain monk thinks the time has come. Now is the right time.

As you well know, the UNESCO charter starts with this phrase: "That since wars begin in the minds of men, it is in the minds of men that the defenses of peace must be constructed." So if war begins in men's minds, solutions for peace begin there as well. Seon meditation teaches that global peace, harmony, and equality—as well as a healthy ecological environment—can be achieved by keeping our minds right and understanding that you and I are not two but one. We must also understand that the same "oneness" exists between the global habitat and the individual; human beings and nature are mutually interdependent.

When you find your true self and reach the home of your mind, you understand the mutual relationship between nature and human beings;

there will be no environmental destruction and ecological damage inflicted only to satisfy greed.

When we find our true selves through meditation, "I" becomes "we"; there is no selfishness or arrogance. Instead, there is a willingness to help others and this planet, our home.

When you find your true self and reach the home of your mind, then there will be no "I'm right, you're wrong." Ignorance will disappear and we will be filled with great wisdom. Confrontation, conflict, and war will disappear and a peaceful world will naturally follow.

So how can we find our true selves then? I believe the answer lies in Ganhwa Seon practice, which I would like to share with you. It can be done by anyone who tastes seawater and says it is salty, or by anyone who tastes honey and says it is sweet. Because this practice is not restricted by an individual character, time, or place, it can be performed during normal daily life and spiritual life.

Everyone lives with a concept of "this is me" and "this is not me." But since this body dies, decays, and returns to nature in less than a hundred years, the physical body cannot be the "true self."

So how can you find your true self? Ask this question, "What is my true self from before I was born?" We have to ask this question again and again. This question is called a hwadu.

You have to question it sincerely, over and over again, putting great effort into questioning continuously. In this state, you will forget how much time passes, what you see or hear, even your own body. This single hwadu question will flow in an intense spiritual concentration called samadhi, with only the hwadu. You will be absorbed in hwadu samadhi for several days or even months. Then one moment when you see an object or hear a sound, your hwadu will suddenly shatter and you will find your true self, arriving to the home of your mind.

Let me illustrate this process, as well as our innate ties with nature, with a story. In ancient China, there was a very famous writer named Su Dongpo. One day he realized the emptiness of all of his fame, talent, and thoughts, and so he decided to dedicate himself to Seon practice. One day, he heard about the brilliant Master Changcong who taught at Xinglong Temple in Mt. Lushan and went to visit him.

After three formal bows, he said, "Master, I came to listen to your

Dharma talk."

But Master Changcong asked him, "How is it that you can only hear the Dharma taught by people, yet you cannot hear the Dharma taught by nature?"

Su Dongpo was astonished by the master's question. Cannot only sentient beings with thoughts and emotions—not non-sentient objects like mountains, rocks, or trees—teach us the truth of Dharma? The degree of his astonishment was the degree of question. As Su Dongpo left the temple and headed to his house, his mind went back to the master's words: "Nature teaches the Dharma?" This questioning filled his whole body as well as his whole mind.

While sitting on his horse's back, Su Dongpo entered the questioning samadhi, the state of absolute and intense focus: "How can non-insentient objects teach the truth? Why can't I hear it?" As his horse went around a corner, he heard the loud sound of the waterfall and was enlightened; he saw the home of his mind! He wrote this verse of enlightenment:

> The roaring of the waterfall expounds 84,000 Buddha's teachings;
> How is this green mountain anything but the body of Buddha?
> In the dark night, the 84,000 teachings—
> How can I show them to everyone the next day?

After that, Su Dongpo enjoyed a blissful life of wisdom. So we must realize that not only the sacred scriptures like the Bible, Koran, and sutras but also nature, stones, and streams teach us truth and wisdom. Once we can hear the non-sentient, we will answer the problems of our ecological crisis that threatens our planet. Genuine world peace will follow.

Brothers and sisters everywhere, the world cries out for healing from radical individualism, which pits one individual against the other, ideology against ideology, and nation and religions against each other—all have threatened the integrity of our planetary environment.

Mountains nurture all kinds of animals and birds; they produce fresh air for people. Water cultivates all kinds of fish and shellfish while providing life for plants and human beings. We must emulate the virtue of mountains, air, and water by nurturing and protecting our home.

The whole world is just one. We must not be seduced by the delusion;

ten thousand different things are not separate from me, nor are they separate from you.

To end this speech, I would like to recite a poem. This is my prayer for eternal peace, happiness, and prosperity in our future.

**It is difficult to distinguish between
The supreme truth and mundane truth.
You must gain the meaning,
Yet forget all words
To come close to the truth.
This one phase of truth
Is bright — so bright — it is one with all phenomena.
Chrysanthemums bloom anew in autumn.**

Thank you for taking the time to listen to my words today.

Become a Fearless Hero:
On the Occasion of Conferring Dharma Ranks

November 22, 2012, at Jogye-sa

Reflect on and wholly revive the moment when you first renounced
the mundane world.

It is neither mind, Buddha, nor a thing.
It is one, two, three, four, five, six, and seven.
Tired, then dwelling on
The tender shoots of early spring tea leaves from India;
Thirsty, then brooding over
Citron picked after the frost from Namhae[9].

Monks and nuns who are receiving the conferral of Dharma ranks today, the passing years are but fleeting moments—it has already been ten, twenty years since you took your monastic vows. Now is the time to reflect upon your practice and progress. Remember that it is only each of you faithfully performing your proper function that will ensure the prosperity of Korean Buddhism. Reflect on and wholly revive the very first moment you aspired to achieve enlightenment, when you first renounced

9 Name of the village in Korea famous for citron fruit; also Master Jinje's hometown.

the mundane world, shaved your heads, and donned the monastic robe. Awaken to your true nature and become a fearless hero—that is the only way you will become worthy of the boundless blessings of the buddhas and patriarchs and repay the generosity of your patrons.

This mountain monk urges you to promulgate Ganhwa Seon far and wide, for Ganhwa Seon is the vessel that can safely sail the treacherous passage over the sea of suffering and carry us to the other shore; it is the crucial shortcut that can conduct us directly to the gate of nirvana. The Buddha flung open the gate of Seon on three occasions of mind-to-mind transmission. The patriarchs of all the ages spread the dazzling display of truth by transmitting luminous wisdom through Seon. And it is in the enlightened truth of the Sixth Patriarch that the Jogye Order found the life source of the buddhaDharma.

Seon Master Shoushan once proclaimed to the assembly:

> Attain the one phrase of the supreme truth and you will be elevated to become the teacher of buddhas and patriarchs. Attain the secondary phrase and you will be honored as the teacher of all beings in heaven and earth. Attain the tertiary phrase and you will barely save yourself.

If someone asks this mountain monk, "What is the one phrase of the supreme truth?" I would say:

Grass grows thick on the tombs of three emperors[10].

If asked, "What is the secondary phrase?" I would reply:

I will not let go of you even if the cudgel snaps off.

To the question, "What is the tertiary phrase?" I would answer:

It is the stake on the roadside to which the donkey is tied.

---

10 Suiren, Fuxi, and Shennong, the legendary Three Sage Kings of ancient China

"Then, from which phrase do you gain wisdom?"

Grasp water, and the moon is in your clutch.
Touch the flower and the clothes are suffused with fragrance.

"What is the act that emerges from enlightenment?"

Pure wind arises in the Seon shrine dedicated to
Winnowing out the Buddha;
The precious moon shines deep under the sea.

"If ten thousand people come, what do you serve them?"

Haeunjeong-sa Temple successfully spreads out ten thousand kinds
of meals and teas;
Ten thousand people from all directions leave satisfied and
transformed.

Our neighbors now come to see this mountain monk in the ardent search for an enlightened Seon teacher. Yet, regrettably, I have yet to meet the rare disciple who has the eyes that see the truth of my teaching, despite my advanced age.

Alas! This mountain monk laments the dearth of disciples who share my aspiration and beneficence to propagate Ganhwa Seon throughout the world.

Monastics in patched robes who receive the conferral today, I hereby make a fervent wish that every one of you, in accordance with your role or level of practice, will pour your heart and soul into upholding Ganhwa Seon and make it flourish so as to merit the immeasurable debt we owe to the buddhas and patriarchs.

Smashing the Cauldron with a Rock

January 1, 2013, at Donghwa-sa

Once you set your mind on seeing your true nature, do not get distracted.

What you see or hear is
Not what is seen or heard.
Sounds or shades are
Not sounds or shades.
Only one more subtle step,
And the six gates brighten up.
It is springtime on earth
In boundless panorama.

If you clearly attain what this mountain monk just said, you will be liberated from all the vicissitudes and afflictions of joy, anger, sorrow, and pleasure of sentient beings and live the life equal to that of the Buddha, eternally blessed with the nirvanic rapture of the supreme truth.

This year, all members of the fourfold community should practice diligently in peace and harmony so that the Seon teachings of Buddha will spread far and wide throughout the Four Seas and Five Lakes.

If we do not resolve this great matter in this lifetime, when can we come across this teaching that leads to liberation? Once you set your mind on seeing your true nature, do not get distracted; persevere to keep your mind steadily on the critical phrase, or hwadu, again and again.

Among those under the tutelage of Seon Master Muzhou, there was a faithful lay practitioner who came to the temple everyday at around the same time.

One day, he arrived later than usual, so Master Muzhou asked him:

"Why did you come so late today?"

"I was late because I was watching the polo match."

"Are players hitting the ball, or the horses?"

"The players were hitting the ball."

"Was the player tired?"

"Yes, he was tired."

"Was the horse tired?"

"Yes, it was."

"Was the mallet also tired?"

The lay practitioner could not offer any answer and returned home speechless. But in the middle of the night, he suddenly awakened to the truth; he received the seal of transmission from the master next day.

What is the meaning of Master Muzhou's asking if the mallet was exhuasted? You should understand this.

Another lay practitioner called Ganzhin brought a wagon full of offerings to the monks following Master Nanquan. After the monks enjoyed the offering, Ganzhin made a request: "Please chant a sutra for me."

The monks together chanted the Heart Sutra, but Ganzhin said, "I did not ask for that sutra."

Of all the nerve! It is indeed difficult to receive the offerings from a patron. What sutra, then, should be chanted?

Master Nanquan's attendant was at the scene and later reported what happened. Upon hearing the story, Master Nanquan immediately stood up and went to the kitchen. On his way to the kitchen, he picked up a large rock and smashed it against a cast iron cauldron used to cook rice.

Why did Master Nanquan destroy the cauldron upon hearing Ganzhin's comment, "I did not ask for that sutra"?

You will deserve the generosity of patrons and be absolved from all debts, generating the capability to melt a thousand pounds of gold a day, if you only grasp the meaning of Master Nanquan's action.

Today is the first day of the year to start the Jogye Order's work anew. Allow me to advise you on how to prepare your body and mind:

First, as disciples of Buddha, all your actions and conduct should be decent and courteous. Second, do not be idle; practice diligently to achieve the wisdom eye to see your true nature so that you can benefit all beings. Third, practice loving-kindness and compassion by generously sharing with neighbors in pain and people in need.

If you embrace the tremendous responsibility of running the Jogye Order with such attitudes in both body and mind, the buddhaDharma will spread and shine all over the world.

Now! Do you know the meaning of Master Nanquan's smashing the caldron with the rock?

Proctor monk!
Starting tomorrow, remove the monks from communal work.
If your mind does not forsake people,
There will be no flicker of shame on your face.

Let Us Forgive and Love One Another

January, 2014, at Jogye-sa

Is the supreme truth of the Dharma present
On this New Year's Day of the Blue Horse year?
It most certainly is.
So what is the truth of the Dharma?
The magnificent glow of the New Year shines brightly forth over the
entire world.
Golden radiance reaches every single village;
Harmonious voices can be heard in every home.
If a tree is attached to its flowers, it is difficult for it to bear fruit.
Rivers must let go of being rivers
In order to become one with the greater sea.
Faced with a future that surges like waves in the ocean,
All past transgressions, feuds, and conflicts that have accumulated
Should be forgotten with each passing year.
Let us aspire collectively for the blissful future of Korea and
Of the entire globe.
Together, let's ascend to fresh, new ground
On the dawn of this auspicious New Year.
Following their own respective duties,
Let ascetics commit themselves to their spiritual practice and
Politicians work for the benefit of the people,
Dedicating their lives to the welfare of all.

When the farmers cultivate the land,
Laborers perform their tasks,
And students strive ardently to learn,
Korea will hear the songs of peace.

The world is one large family, and its infinite manifestations are but one body, not separate from any of us. How could we possibly make distinctions between the north and the south or the east and the west?

Life is most rare and precious, and the laws of cause and effect clearly demonstrate how enmity and resentment return when one repays life's generosity with malice. We must understand how holding grudges is infinite and without end. Let us forgive and love one another.

Water nurtures all sentient beings, but when its path is blocked, it must gather itself to push through.

Nothing is as humble and smooth as water when it flows, but there is also nothing more powerful when it encounters something strong and immovable.

Abundance results in all creation, with a temperament of everlasting modesty and reservation of water.

During the year of the blue horse, let virtues flow like water in aiding those who are suffering. Prevent bickering between neighbors and treat all as if our own; foster love and forgiveness to swiftly bring unification to Korea and the realization of world peace.

It is said that "People are impoverished when they lack wisdom; the horse gets enfeebled and its hair gets long."

If we aspire for every birth to be victorious and blissful, we must hold the following hwadu in our daily lives: "What is my true self from before I was born?"

With strong, unceasing doubt, we must discover our true self. With great wisdom found from our true self and the supreme blessing and virtue seen within, let us all enjoy eternal bliss and freedom together.

WALKING THE PATH:
SEON PRACTICE

Taking Steps Toward the Great Truth: Approaching the 3-Month Retreat

December 1, 2012, at Haeunjeong-sa

Seeking the truth of the buddhaDharma is pursuing the great path. Practice means treading this great path toward truth. The truth of the great path is unfathomable, limitlessly vast, and free from all duality—right and wrong, good and bad. It is a state in which all differentiation by shape and color ceases to exist. This is the ethereal place we aspire to reach, yet it eludes us. It is like trying to grasp empty space.

We cannot but question whether or not we are ready to embark on this arduous journey. Most vitally important for us to walk this path is having the correct attitude. Infinitely deep faith and ferocious courage reaching the sky are keys to attaining enlightenment. If you possess these mental qualities, attaining enlightenment is as easy as touching your nose while washing your face. Yet it can be like plucking a star out of the sky unless you encounter the correct Dharma and invest sincere belief in it.

Anyone who develops genuine faith can practice Dharma. Devotedly follow the instructions from enlightened teachers who have successfully walked this path ahead of you. If you do not go astray and wander off the course indicated by your teachers, you will reach and enter the gates of truth with relative ease. However, if you are blinded by conceit and led by false views, there will be no progress, even after several lifetimes of hard practice. The truth of the great path lies beyond the realm of speech, beyond the mind that distinguishes and discriminates. One must rise above such false views to attain the state of "no-mind."

Achieving the state of no-mind is not as difficult as one may imagine. The doors to the great path open wide for anyone truly ready to discard their own body and life as Huike, the Second Patriarch of the Chinese Chan lineage, did. To prove his desperate resolve to attain the Dharma, he stood in a howling snowstorm all night long and then cut off his own arm. It was his sincere faith and fierce devotion that earned Huike the transmission of the Dharma from the First Patriarch, Bodhidharma. Some people dedicate their whole lives to practicing Seon, only to accomplish little or nothing. Probably 90% of the time, the reason is not because they receive incorrect teachings but because they do not yearn and seek for the truth desperately enough. They just sit around, wasting time in pursuing pointless thoughts. If you investigate a hwadu with a fervent determination to resolve this matter of life and death in this very life—at any cost—you will not notice the passage of time. You will not notice people making a racket around you. You will even forget you are sitting in meditation. Only one thought will remain. When this hwadu single-mindedness begins to flow unceasingly, your eyes will open to the truth. This is true for everyone, without exception.

Therefore, the first thing to do is firmly establish the correct mindset. All the agitations of the mind stirred by external stimuli should be severed at once, as if slashed with a single swift stroke of a sword. All trifling concerns of the body—whether your body is sick or not, or has enough to eat—should all be dismissed at once. Focus your entire mind and life energy into your hwadu investigation. If you do, then other thoughts cannot arise, even if you try. Your mind should be completely filled with only the thought of the hwadu, so full that there is no space for anything else. It should be similar to when a sensitive part of your flesh is suddenly pricked by a needle and your whole attention is occupied by that pain. Your mind should focus on your hwadu that much. Your mind should be so captivated by the hwadu that other people may think you are crazy or even possessed.

Your single-minded focus on the hwadu will run like flowing water for days, months, even years. You will forget everything. Then, when the causes and conditions dictated by your karma are right, the hwadu will shatter to reveal the place where truth lies.

When winter comes, the freezing wind cuts and slashes at the body. However, before we know it, a balmy breeze ushers in spring, and the bitter cold goes away. Then all things burst back to life. If your efforts are honest and sincere, hwadu practice is no different from nature; it will bear fruit just as nature does. However, if a practitioner's questioning does not arise from the bottom of his or her heart, this ever-flowing one-mindedness will not come, even after ten, twenty, or thirty years of ceaseless effort. If this is the case, you will not find your true nature. If your questioning of the hwadu is poignantly heartfelt and you keep investigating it until it cuts to the bone, however, three months in retreat will pass before you know it.

Some practitioners may go stir crazy while cut off from the world and cooped up in the temple, craving news from the outside. This is not the correct mindset for a practitioner. Such a person, no matter how long he practice, is just pretending. It does not matter if he keeps trying until his hair turns white. Such a bogus practice will bring no benefit. He will only waste his patrons' donations, amassing a huge karmic debt; when he nears death, he will feel only regret. A practitioner must have the right mindset first. Otherwise, no matter how long you stay a monk, whether it is ten, twenty, or thirty years, or until your hair turns white, it will be the same dance to the same tune.

When I examine Seon practitioners these days, I cannot tell whether they are sleeping or investigating a hwadu. I no longer see a practitioner penetrating a hwadu and generating a sense of doubt so intense it pierces bone. I no longer see in them the fierce spirit essential to the practice.

You are monks who renounced the world. If you are bored after only one three-month retreat, shame on you. If you cannot wait for the retreat to end when you can wander off into the mountains again with your travel sack slung over your shoulder, as a monk in tattered robes, you should be embarrassed.

Imagine that your home was suddenly invaded and your parents, sisters, and brothers were all butchered. Now you are the only survivor looking at the carnage. How would you feel? If you feel like that when you work on your hwadu, torpor and delusion cannot even come near. If that is how you investigate your hwadu, I can guarantee you will penetrate it within three years.

If you are ordained monastics, you should search your soul everyday and ask yourself whether you have spent the day sincerely trying to see your true nature, or whether you are just squandering your patrons' donations. Arouse the ardent aspiration again and again. If you fulfill your role as a monk, you will help save all beings; if you fail, you cannot save even yourself. It is you who renounced the secular world and chose this path. You did not do it for your parents. You did not do it for anyone else. Abandon all conditional external things and the mental confusion they cause. If you cannot shrug off all falsehoods and fabrications, you cannot progress a single step.

Revive the firm resolve you aroused when you first decided to give up all worldly pleasures, when you turned your back to them. You should give up trying to be a respectable citizen; instead, you should become a complete fool who thinks, walks, and breathes only your hwadu. If the hwadu is the only thing that fills your mind, nothing will bother you. Whether this three-month retreat starts or ends will not matter. Eating and sleeping will no longer concern you. Even your body will become irrelevant. You will exist in this state for some time, but you will find yourself nearer to the gate of the great path. Eventually, you will throw that gate wide open.

The same goes for lay Buddhists. You will not come into a big windfall of merit nor suddenly become a better meditator just by crisscrossing the country visiting this and that temple. Make the resolution now: "The only thing I must do is to find the bright light of the mind!" Do not waver from it. Cast off all affectations and expunge all attachments to any perceptions that arise from contact with the external world. Learn how to investigate your hwadu and persist in it.

If you are married and have children, you do need to take care of your family. However, if you assiduously persevere in your hwadu investigation while living the secular life, all unwholesome habits and persistent misconceptions of the mind will fade away.

The hwadu "What is the true self from before I was born?" is excellent for any Seon practitioner.

We must discover the true self, no matter who we are, because we have been lucky enough to encounter the buddhaDharma in this life. Don't you want to cheerfully shuck off your body and make a glorious exit from this life when death is near? The true self is the true master of this body born of our parents. This true self is the one that does the talking, the coming and going in our everyday lives. This true self is listening to this Dharma talk right now. This true self never leaves us throughout our lives, not even a second. Yet we do not know it and do not seek to attain it. This is the height of stupidity. How can you not resolve to find it? If you engender, through unrelenting questioning of a hwadu, a doubt so overpowering that it penetrates bone and twists your insides, your practice will ripen before you know it.

If the hwadu "What is my true self from before I was born?" is sharply imprinted onto a single thought, and if this single thought is vividly present in the mind at all times and in all places—whether coming or going, cooking or cleaning, working or sleeping—all the unhealthy habits you have accumulated life after life will completely melt away. Once this state is reached, the mind will attain enlightenment whether you are a monk or a lay person, whether you want it or not.

You do not have to travel to the moon or to heaven to bring back the buddhaDharma to this earth. In the heart of every sentient being lives the original mind. The mind of sentient beings is, even here and now, no different from that of the buddhas or the patriarchs, not even by a hair's breadth. But sentient beings are too deluded to know the truth.

If you practice diligently and experience your original mind, you will rise to a status equal to the Buddha. Your replies to gongans, which the buddhas and patriarchs have generously left to us, will flow effortlessly and fluently. That is why enlightened teachers use the gongans of past masters to verify the attainment of practitioners. Truly awakened beings will point to east when asked which direction is the east, and point to west when asked which direction is the west. They will turn west when the teacher is pointing east. But if they have not penetrated the gates of truth, those whose eyes are not yet open do not know east from west. Their answers are confusing; the gongan exchange becomes chaotic. If you fail to forsake your misguided opinions, you acquire a perverted view, which is of no assistance on the great path. You have to be wary of such views, for once you become ensnared in them, you will fall victim to them, not only in this life, but every time you are reborn a human.

Therefore, practitioners must have absolute confidence in their enlightened teacher, unfalteringly relying on his guidance and training to acquire correct insight. You can cultivate the causes and conditions that will bring you closer to the great path only if you immediately let go of your wrong views when your teacher shows you the error of your ways.

You should check to see if there are weaknesses in your mind that may hold you back on this great path. You must question your hwadu until it is carved into your bones.

All monks have renounced this world in order to seek their true nature and attain enlightenment.

The first thing Shakyamuni Buddha said after becoming enlightened was, "If I enter parinirvana right now, without uttering a single word of Dharma, it would still be better than twenty-one days of unremitting reflection and deliberation." This was the greatest teaching of all, a teaching that none of the thousands of saints nor tens of thousands of buddhas preceding Shakyamuni Buddha had managed to deliver.

However, Manjusri was at Shakyamuni Buddha's side and begged him, "World-Honored One, Dharma is indeed such to a truly enlightened saint, but beings of lesser spiritual capacity are in desperate need of understandable Dharma, and therefore, your elucidation." Thus, Shakyamuni Buddha was obliged to dedicate forty-nine more years of his life to teaching Dharma to sentient beings. At his parinirvana, Shakyamuni Buddha told the sangha gathered around him, "For the past forty-nine years, I have given different teachings to different people, each teaching attuned to the faculties and capacities of the listener. Yet in all that time, I have not imparted a single word of the buddhaDharma."

When you finally attain truth, you will realize that the spectacular array of teachings the Buddha gave for forty-nine years were mere skillful means to placate crying babies.

Now, what should we do to be awakened to our true nature and attain enlightenment? The answer is to practice with a living phrase. Enlightened masters of the past stressed the importance of practicing with a living phrase. They said, "Make sure to practice only with living phrases, and never with a dead one," or "Practice with a living phrase and become a teacher to the buddhas and patriarchs themselves."

Investigating a dead phrase will certainly never lead anyone to awakening; it is not even enough to save yourself. The difference between a living phrase and a dead phrase is as vast as the distance from earth to heaven.

Then, what is a living phrase? You are practicing with a living phrase only when you penetrate "the one phrase at the crown of a thousand enlightened beings." Otherwise, you have no idea what the world of the living phrase is about. It is said that if you break through the world of living phrases, you will become a teacher to buddhas and patriarchs themselves. If you are a spiritual seeker worth your salt, your goal should be to penetrate "the one phrase at the crown of a thousand enlightened beings" and become an enlightened teacher who thoroughly masters a dazzling array of unhindered manifestations of truth, spontaneously saving life while killing it, or giving the truth while taking it away.

However, a dead phrase is contaminated with intellectual learning and knowledge, mired in deluded distinctions and discriminations. Your eyes are not opened yet; far from enabling you to freely and fully embody manifest truth, a dead phrase will not even save yourself.

You must pour your heart and soul into becoming an exemplary teacher with both consummate learning and practice, one that can teach even a thousand saints.

We all have eyes, nose, mouth, and ears, just like the buddhas and patriarchs. Likewise, there is no reason we cannot attain the same enlightenment if we cultivate in ourselves great courage and great faith. Sages of all generations said, "The greater the doubt, the greater the enlightenment." Once great doubt is generated, it will trigger a true sense of questioning. This in turn will eventually encase the whole world in a dense mass of doubt. Then, your hwadu will be shattered.

How do we advance our investigation with great courage and great faith? The only way is to meet a radiant-eyed enlightened teacher, learn from him or her how to correctly investigate the hwadu, then fervently and ferociously endeavor to shatter the hwadu at all hours, whether awake or asleep.

We have been so busy playing as sentient beings through countless lifetimes and countless eons that it is difficult to grasp a hwadu firmly in our mind. At first, the hwadu appears to be ten thousand miles away. If the strength of your aspiration is just mediocre, it cannot overcome the combined momentum of habits, afflictions, and delusions compounded through your past lives. Only the soaring valor of an exalted hero can conquer the overwhelming power of karmic energies to attain this path, the very best of all paths leading to one's true nature. Let go of all your attractions to the external world of sensory perceptions and try again and again, with all your might, until your mind is entirely and singularly focused on your hwadu. Once this intense state of hwadu single-mindedness is achieved, your hwadu will be shattered in your own time, determined by your own karma. You will arrive at the land of the Tathagata, still seated on your meditation cushion.

The Correct Way of Practicing Seon

Seon practice leads us to the home of the mind. But what is Seon practice? What is the world of enlightenment like?

Every human being has a mind. It is with us always. Fundamentally, there is no difference whatsoever between the mind of a Buddha and those of sentient beings. However, while the Buddha's mind radiates unobstructed brilliant light, the minds of sentient beings are shrouded in the shadow of delusions cast by the dark clouds of affliction. The minds of sentient beings are hazy, bogged down in a quagmire of raging afflictions that lash out in a thousand, even ten thousand directions, driven by their karma. Countless distracting thoughts and feelings of arrogance, egotism, envy, jealousy, greed, affection, fear, and anxiety whirl and howl furiously in our minds, denying us even a single moment of rest.

If we practice Seon consistently in our everyday lives, all defilements will dissipate and the mind's natural luminosity will inevitably be revealed. We will feel joyful and lighthearted, achieving everything we set our mind to because all karmic hindrances have been dissolved.

We can all reach the home of the mind within this lifetime if we meet a "bright-eyed, enlightened teacher" and faithfully follow his or her guidance. Furthermore, we will be reborn into a wonderfully rewarding life in our next incarnation.

The home of the mind, revealed by Seon practice, is infinite. Centuries ago, people described it as being as immense as Changan, an ancient Chinese capital. Tens of millions of households inhabit it, just as millions of people inhabit such places as Seoul or New York. There are infinite buddhas and bodhisattvas in the Changan of our mind as well, but contained in it are innumerable planes of existence, each of them just as expansive as Changan.

The boundless megalopolis of our mind harbors within it an infinite number of colossal cities, each one just as big as Changan. Knock on any door and ask, "Is anybody home?" Shakyamuni Buddha and Maitreya will answer. Go to the next door and knock again; Manjusri and Samantabhadra will be waiting. Amitabha Buddha and Ksitigarbha also walk the street. In the home of our mind, buddhas, buddhanature, and the bodhi mind are omnipresent in all their glorious perfection.

Seon is sublime and subtle like this. When enlightened, we see that the six realms do not exist separately, that ordinary men and extraordinary sages are not two. When enlightened, samsara is instantly transformed into the kingdom of the Buddha; 84,000 afflictions disappear without a trace.

In the home of the mind, the whole universe emits a golden glow, and plants and trees radiate a balmy light. The air resonates with the music of prajna as the birds sing songs of wisdom. We must claim this realm as our own; otherwise, we will never extricate ourselves from the dilemma of life and death.

To die is only to change bodies, much like changing clothes. Enlightened people do not concern themselves with the approach of death. Even at the last moment, they are supremely unworried and undaunted because they know that in truth, nothing is ever created or destroyed.

In the fall, the sky is often perfectly clear, without even a speck of a cloud to spoil its clarity. However, if our eyes are rubbed or hit hard, flashes of flower-like images flicker in our eyes, blurring our vision. Sometimes, we even see stars. To us, they look exactly like stars; our senses register them as real. However, the fact that we see the stars does not make them real. They are just optical illusions. Life and death exist only because we fail to see reality, blinded by the phantom images of non-existent flowers.

If we return to the home of the mind by practicing Seon, we will be unimpeded by figments of our imagination and see the reality of the truth. Having seen our true self, we will no longer be tainted by the world. The essence of the truth is so exquisitely radiant and pure that those who fully embrace and embody it are defiled by nothing, standing dignified and gloriously alone.

It is difficult for contemporary society to comprehend such perfection, but there are numerous stories of masters who enjoyed this great freedom, liberated from all attachment to life and death.

Once there lived in China a renowned Seon Master named Lanzan. The emperor, hearing of Lanzan's reputation, wanted to invite him to give a Dharma talk, so he dispatched a messenger.

When the messenger reached Master Lanzan's cave, the master was burning a huge heap of dried cow and horse manure. He then roasted taro over the fire and ate them. The messenger bowed three times and said, "I am here to accompany you to the emperor's court as his honored guest."

Master Lanzan, however, took no heed and just continued to eat taro. The messenger was shocked because in his long career as the imperial envoy, no one had ever responded with such a lack of interest to the emperor's summons. The messenger pleaded with the master to come with him to the palace, but Master Lanzan remained utterly indifferent. The messenger had no choice but to give up and return to the palace. The emperor, however, sent the messenger again to Master Lanzan. When the messenger arrived at the master's cave, he was still in the same unwashed rags from days before. He was filthy with grime and still eating roasted taro, snot streaming from his nose. The messenger was incredulous. How could this man be the illustrious Master Lanzan esteemed by the whole country? Disgusted, the messenger chided the master, "I am here on behalf of the emperor himself. How dare you treat me like this? Can you at least wipe your nose while you are eating?"

"What rubbish! Why should I wipe my nose for the likes of you?" The master brushed him off and would not give him the time of day. The messenger's mouth gaped speechless. Talking to an imperial envoy in this manner was an offense serious enough to put a person in prison. However, it was impossible to change Master Lanzan's mind.

The messenger again returned empty handed, but the emperor would not take no for an answer and ordered the messenger to bring the master back at any cost. At that time, defying the emperor's command three times was punishable by death. Even a recluse who forsook the world and lived in a cave such as Master Lanzan knew this. When the messenger showed up a third time, the master stopped eating taro and stretched his neck out saying, "Cut off my head and take it back with you."

This is a marvelous example of great freedom unhindered by even matters of life and death. A paragon of spiritual attainment such as Master Lanzan should be a tremendous inspiration to practitioners everywhere. How can we cultivate such a capacity to transcend life and death?

If we practice Seon and arrive at the home of the mind, we will rise above form and appearance and transcend life and death. I hear that many self-help programs and therapies popular these days make liberal use of the phrase "emptying the mind." This can be misleading. The mind can never be emptied simply because we will it to. That should be obvious if we probed a little deeper.

Sentient beings are ensnared in layer upon layer of habits amassed and acquired through countless lifetimes. Men lust after beautiful women; women seek the attention of successful men. People desire money and crave nice things. As a result, our minds are never truly calm; we are constantly troubled by jealousy, fear, anxiety, and other disruptive emotions. These emotions are neither good nor bad. They are just tendencies we pick up as we go round and round through the vicissitudes of the six realms, sometimes as humans and sometimes as animals. They will not vanish simply because we decide one day that "I will stop doing it," or "I will empty my mind." They can be transformed only through the hardships of arduous training and life's bitter experiences.

We are now standing at the gate of an infallible path: Seon. It generates a mind singly focused on questioning hwadu, directing us to investigate the truth. Such a mind will transcend all conditioned distinctions, including the distinction between internal and external. In this state of mind, death is nothing, and we become no different from a statue or a corpse. It is only when we are renewed and reborn in this realm of mind that we can truly attain "no-mind" and— regardless of pleasant or unpleasant circumstances—stop generating discursive thoughts.

What, then, is the correct way of practicing Seon? First, sit comfortably with the back straight and the shoulders open. Sit squarely and securely. Otherwise, if you sit for a long time, the back slouches and the chest sinks in. If you lose the correct posture, it will be difficult to maintain the state of deep concentration and clear headedness required for hwadu investigation. Even a one-hour meditation will feel very long, dull, and dreary.

Second, once you achieve the correct posture, hold your hwadu in your mind with your eyes turned downward, focused about two meters in front of you on the floor. Keep your eyes open. If you hold your hwadu at eye level, it causes tension and your chi will rise upward. This pooling of chi, or energy, in the head induces headache and a feeling of heaviness, making practice impossible. It is one of the mistakes beginners commonly make.

Third, if you have received a hwadu from an enlightened teacher, devote yourself to it wholly and fervently. This is the most crucial part of Seon practice. Those who are fortunate enough to meet an enlightened teacher and receive a hwadu must cherish and cultivate it ardently and avidly. If you do not have a hwadu, use the hwadu "What is the true self from before I was born?" or "Ten thousand Dharmas return to the one; where does the one return to?" A third popular hwadu is, "The cypress tree in front of the Dharma Hall," which was delivered in reply to the question, "What is the meaning of Bodhidharma's coming from the West?"

If you hold your hwadu dearly and desperately, like parents longing for the only son born after three generations who then met a sudden and untimely death, torpor and discursive thoughts will vanish. Such delusional hindrances arise only because the mind is not yet thoroughly and resolutely latched onto the single point of the hwadu. Remind yourself, "How incredibly lucky I am to encounter this precious buddhaDharma! I must awaken to my true nature in this lifetime." Then, dedicate yourself to your hwadu. Afterward, not only will your mind be free of lethargy and dullness, but all afflictive thoughts and sensory phenomena that mercilessly dictate your life will no longer have any hold on you.

When we are lost in deep thought, we often become blind and deaf to what is going on around us, even when we are eating or talking with family. If you immerse yourself in practice even more intensely than that, rapt in examining and questioning the hwadu, it completely severs sight and sound; only the questioning of hwadu remains. Time passes in the twinkle of an eye, and only your single-minded focus will remain, rushing and flowing like a stream.

This practice will work for all people, monastics as well as the laity. If all you do while sitting on the meditation cushion is think about sons, daughters, husbands, wives, or house chores, giving rise to all sorts of illusions, you are just wasting your time. Monks and nuns must be careful too. This single-mindedness cannot be maintained if one's attention is sidetracked even for a second by thoughts of food, clothes, or any bodily discomforts. One's mind should be thoroughly absorbed in hwadu investigation. Whether sitting or standing, cleaning the temple or tending the vegetable garden, whatever the physical body is doing, the mind should wrestle with the hwadu at all times. Soldier on with your hwadu practice, and before you know it, all delusions will subside and distracting thoughts will no longer find a toehold in your mind.

If you lack such fervent devotion and urgency, and you take up Seon practice just to mimic others, the hwadu will escape you; sitting meditation will be torturous and tedious. It will bear no genuine fruit.

Fourth, offer your sincere aspiration to the Buddha every morning and evening, saying, "May my one-mindedness focused on the hwadu continue ceaselessly so that I will attain the great enlightenment." Making such an aspiration every day is one of the keys to achieving this noble task in this life, as it offsets the negative effects of one's habits and flaws.

That is why no past masters ever neglected making this vow when they practiced: "May I be granted the blessing of meeting a truly enlightened teacher, transcend life and death upon hearing his words of wisdom, and attain enlightenment so that I can spread the Buddha's teaching and save all beings."

Buddhas and patriarchs of the past, and even to this day, all attained Buddhahood by relying absolutely on the strength of their vows. It is your vow that will carry you over the great path, whether you are a striving young monk or an enthusiastic lay practitioner.

Fix it firmly in your mind that your ardent aspiration, together with wholehearted faith and fierce effort, should always be present when you are engaged in hwadu investigation. It is the only way to overcome all obstacles and maintain the smooth and constant flow of single-minded focus on the hwadu. Once a steady and stable flow of one-mindedness is established, anyone can see the radiant light of the original mind. When the gates of the mind are thrown open, all 84,000 kinds of wisdoms appear, perfectly formed and ready to be used. Anyone can immediately attain the capacities of the Buddha.

Once you learn the proper sitting posture and how to hold the hwadu correctly, investigate the hwadu unceasingly, whether sitting or standing, working or resting. Do not limit your practice only to sitting meditation. This is a practice that should grow and mature in daily life. You are not cultivating it correctly if you only investigate it in sitting meditation, and it eludes you whenever you move. You will need it more desperately when you are beset by hardship, near death, or in extreme pain. You should be able to hold the hwadu unwaveringly, not only when your mind is calm and relaxed but also in any adverse situation.

We learn sitting meditation first because it is the easiest way to get used to Seon practice. Once you are more experienced with sitting meditation, make sure you focus on the hwadu while going about your everyday activities. Let it develop and mature while eating, talking, or working in the office, until your complete focus on the hwadu flows like a neverending powerful current of water, twenty-four hours a day. Only then will the practice yield true results.

Life is short. Time slips by, and before you know it, you are already old. Your body grows weak and sick, and death approaches. You finally look back on your life and realize, "I have wasted my life!" Then it is too late. What is the use of regret at that point? We practice Seon to be forever free from the suffering of life and death. Your practice today determines the causes and conditions of your next life. Don't be idle. You cannot afford to waste even a second.

Start here and now. Pour your heart and soul into cultivating sincere faith and developing doubt through questioning a hwadu, minute by minute, hour by hour. Once hwadu single-mindedness starts flowing, you will forget the sense of seeing and hearing, even time itself. This state of mind may last one week, a month, or even a full year, flowing like a perpetual stream. This is the samadhi of one thought. Let it flow. Your time will come in accordance with causes and conditions. The door of truth will open wide to reveal your true self.

Even if you are lucky enough to be reborn as a human for tens of thousands of consecutive lifetimes, it is a rare opportunity to be initiated into a genuine Seon practice. It is even rarer to receive a correct teaching on how to practice Seon. That is why the ancient sages emphasized, "Sentient beings are entrapped in a frantic maze of bad habits amassed while repeating innumerable cycles of life and death. These bad habits make it extremely difficult for them to be introduced to the true Dharma." Now you have been launched onto this precious path. Practice hard now, and revel in the bliss and joy of the true Dharma every time you are reborn as a human being.

My words are wasted if you do not put them into action. Start practicing Seon right away. Sit down, turn and face the wall, and check if your posture is correct. Turn your gaze downward and place your hwadu about two meters in front of you. Then, put your entire mind into it; generate doubt.

When you nurture the investigation of your hwadu and generate doubt, be sure to hold your hwadu clearly and in its entirety. Even if your practice starts out clear and sharp, it often grows dim as discursive thoughts arise. This happens quite often to beginners. If you notice it, carefully gather up your hwadu in its entirety and start over. Just keep trying. There will come a moment when true doubt suddenly appears; a single thought will come alive and start flowing. This is what authentic practice is all about.

With your single thought running clear and bright, your doubt will grow all-consuming. As your doubt deepens, the hwadu in its totality will flow like a stream of water. When your hwadu single-mindedness becomes that constant, you will no longer be swayed by what you see and what you hear. Soon you will attain enlightenment.

Questions to Master Jinje on Seon

ENLIGHTENMENT

1. What is enlightenment?

Enlightenment means to see the mind, to see the true self that is the essence of the mind. When you attain your fundamentally awakened state, you will eventually understand all the 84,000 Dharmas. To one who is truly enlightened to the nature of mind, all things are free from discrimination, which means that the infinite variety things are simply one. It is as if ten people see a thing clearly in the light of day, but at night they all see it differently. Therefore if you view the mind through its natural effulgence, everything is perfectly clear: there is no right or wrong, good or evil, merit or demerit.

2. What is an awakened one?

Someone who has awakened to his or her true nature is simply a person whose lives the truth and guides all people to live in peace.

3. What difference does it make in our lives if we attain enlightenment?

If you are enlightened, then everyday life flows in harmony with the truth, entirely of its own accord. You will live a simple life: when you're thirsty, you drink; when you're hungry, you eat. But people in this world are always looking for something special, even though there is nothing particularly mystical or "special" about truth itself. If you do not discriminate between self or others, and do not give rise to feelings of arrogance, pride, envy, jealousy, and conflict, then you will live a life of equanimity, enthusiasm, stability, and impartiality, treating the whole world as a single family. This kind of life is the way and the realm of truth.

If you realize the truth, you will live in bliss every day. There will be nothing more special than drinking tea when you're thirsty, resting when you're tired, or greeting guests when they visit. These everyday acts will be enough.

BIRTH AND DEATH

4. We all understand why living in the world might bring suffering, but what is the biggest suffering of all?

Birth-and-death is the biggest one.

5. For sentient beings, birth-and-death may well be the biggest matter. But what is death?

If you understand the true self, you come to know that death is but a flower in the sky; it is just like an optical illusion. You know how, when you are struck suddenly on your head, or something hits on or near your eye, phantom flowers arise like a flash of lightning? Those "flowers" are not real things, but just false, illusory images that flit here and there because of momentary eye trouble. "Birth-and-death" is just like this.

6. And yet we fear death. And shouldn't we?

If you are afraid of death, you do not know the true path.

7. How can those of us who are still unenlightened conquer the fear of death?

All sentient beings have a fear of death. But if you are steady in your Seon meditation as you seek to find your true self in our daily life, you will gain the power of samadhi (concentration). Then when you see your true identity through the power of this insight, all fears, anxieties, and illusions will vanish in an instant. At the moment of death, you will leave your body with a clear and composed mind.

8. I was told that Buddhism teaches about rebirth. Is there really rebirth?

If you realize the true nature of reality, there is nothing to be reborn into the six rebirth destinies. But beings who are unenlightened will surely experience rebirth.

9. In Buddhism, sometimes we hear such adages as "birth and death are not separate," or "originally, there is no birth and no death." How do you distinguish between these two teachings?

The reason for birth and the reason for death are the same; that is why we say that birth and death are not two. However, in the ultimate dimension, originally there is no birth or death.

CONDITIONS FOR THE PRACTICE OF SEON

10. Is there any difference in the extent to which monks or nuns and lay Buddhists can practice Seon?

Buddhist monks and nuns have a lighter daily burden, since they are single and have no family obligations. Lay Buddhists have a heavier burden to carry in their practice, since they have families to support and to worry about. However, if you have devout faith in your practice, there should be no obstacle whatsoever. With a thoroughgoing attitude and a devout faith in seeking the right way, through effort and perseverance you can eventually meet a clear-eyed enlightened one to guide and inspire your meditation. It doesn't matter whether you are a monk or a layperson: you will live truly according to your occupation in the world.

11. Can we make progress in practice without keeping the precepts?

In order to accomplish the great way, keeping the precepts is a very important foundation. You will become enlightened only if you continue questioning your hwadu while also single-mindedly keeping the pure precepts. If you can practice like this, then all at once bright wisdom unfolds while singled-minded absorption (samadhi) develops. It is for this reason that the Buddha taught the three-fold path of morality, meditative absorption, and wisdom. These three are actually not separate things: they are one. If you can fulfill all these three aspects, then you are certain to become a sage.

PRACTICE, PRAYER, AND WISDOM

12. Is hwadu practice done through one's own effort, or by relying on others?

The practice of meditation is absolutely accomplished through one's own effort. No one can do your meditation for you. You have to devote your own energies to meditation practice. When intense, determined concentration continues on the hwadu question, the hwadu will shatter by itself, quite suddenly and without outside intervention.

13. What do you think of prayers and mantra recitation?

The repetition of prayers, dharanis, and mantras are also important spiritual work. People of lower spiritual capacity can come to the door of Mahayana (the "Greater Vehicle") through devotion.

14. Tell us about virtue.

If you do not speak ill of others and make yourself equal to anyone according to your pure nature—free from self-centeredness and arrogance—you will be respected as a virtuous one.

15. What is wisdom?

When you see into the nature of your mind, your mind's radiance will shine brightly. When your mind becomes bright, that is what we call "wisdom."

16. Even though sentient beings are ignorant and shrouded in delusive karmic consciousness, they have observed the universe and developed the various sciences and technologies that have led to many practical improvements in people's everyday lives. Is this different from wisdom?

"Wisdom" and "knowledge" are two different things. While wisdom is cultivated by looking into the original nature of your minds and recovering its inherent radiance, worldly knowledge is based on discriminating between mental concepts and configuring different things. Science results from accumulating such worldly knowledge.

KARMA

17. What is karma?

To those acquainted with truth, everything they meet is the true law. But to sentient beings with no insight into the truth that lies inside their own minds, everything turns into habits and karma.

18. When does karma appear?

The first thought that turns against the reality of your own original nature leads inexorably to all other deluded thoughts. If you are focused on the samadhi inherent in your original nature, deluded thoughts will never arise; but as soon as even a single thought leads you astray, an infinite variety of thoughts follow. That is karma.

19. How can we break through karmic obstacles?

Though you can get rid of a portion of your karmic obstacles by repentance practices and ceremonies, the only way to completely sever the cord of karmic delusion is by breaking through to enlightenment.

20. Is it true that sensory experience only adds things to our karmic storehouse?

Yes, it is. If you see and hear many things, your thoughts also increase accordingly, and those thoughts will grow into habits that eventually strengthen your karmic cognition.

21. Then is it good enough just to practice in the remote mountains without indulging in sensory cognition?

No, it is not that simple. Without an enlightened master, you only waste your precious time and energy. So a wise seeker after the truth always goes to see an enlightened master to enquire after the right path of meditation practice.

MISCELLANEOUS QUESTIONS ON SEON

22. Is your stage of enlightenment the same as that of Shakyamuni Buddha, who awoke to his own nature 2,500 years ago by suddenly seeing the morning star?

Enlightenment means that you have seen your original nature. Shakyamuni Buddha got enlightened by seeing his own nature, and all the other awakened ones are exactly the same. Since there is no discrimination in the ground of true enlightenment, if anyone claims to have been enlightened on his own without a master, he will be called a devil, a deviant from the true teachings. For this reason, the Buddha insisted that we need to receive certification from a master who inherited the right Dharma flawlessly, and there can never be such a cock of the walk who insists on self-claimed enlightenment. In order to leave no room for manipulation or lies in the field of enlightenment, we keep up the tradition of receiving certification from an enlightened predecessor.

23. What is the reason for Bodhidharma coming from India to China?

He had no intention.

24. Why did he have no intention?

AAUUK!

EXAMINE YOUR HWADU

25. On one level, it would seem that the Buddha's teaching is easy to understand since he had to appeal to people from every walk of life. However, your teaching—as well as some other patriarchs' gongan instructions—is too difficult to understand and generates no real questioning, or doubt. What should I do to penetrate those gongan

teachings in order to see the world of truth with ease?

My words, as well as all the patriarchs' teachings, are as sharp as an arrow. Just as the Buddha consoled crying babies with various expedients out of his compassion, so too his forty-nine years of teachings are only a guidebook; they are not a real teaching. The patriarchs' teachings, to the contrary, are like a sharp arrow that pierces straight to the heart. Teachings such as this drive practitioners deeper and deeper into their sense of questioning or doubt. If students hear these words and can keep this single-mindedness of questioning, then any and all karmic forces will fade away over time. Therefore any student who is truly engaged in this meditation should consider an ancient master's single sentence or half a phrase as a piece of gold. You should have pure faith in those statements, do as they instruct, and take their guidance deeply to heart.

Nevertheless, should you be conniving and skeptical like a wild fox, even a hundred years of intensive practice will bring no benefit. But, when you meet an enlightened one, with thorough faith you should receive what you are taught, and practice consistently with an upright mental attitude.

If a practitioner empties his mind and receives the full guidance of an enlightened one, he takes the master's treasure as his own. That is why, in order to step into the gate of the great way, you should throw away all your narrow understanding and knowledge. Please don't hear this story carelessly but take it deeply to heart. Put it into practice, and you will surely gain a lot.

26. What is "Ganhwa Seon"?

"Ganhwa Seon" means the meditation practice (Seon) that investigates or questions (gan) a great topic of inquiry (hwa). These topics are often taken from a case (gongan) appearing in the classical collections of Seon literature, especially the dialogues between masters and their students. This is the meditation practice inherited from Shakyamuni Buddha and transmitted down to later generations of patriarchs up to the present generation. Ganhwa Seon has at its core this deep, earnest questioning.

27. What is the hwadu?

The reality publicly shown to all people by all the buddhas and enlightened masters is the hwadu ("topic") and the gongan ("case").

28. Nowadays, some say that the hwadu is just a preparatory method, a way to prepare the mind for practice. What is your view on this?

If you practice hwadu questioning and realize it completely, then it will be a shortcut to the truth.

29. How can I receive a hwadu?

First do three full prostrations, empty your thoughts, and listen to the enlightened master's instructions.

30. In the past, when great masters gave a hwadu phrase to a student, they considered the receiver's capability first. But in these days, it seems like some masters just pass out hwadus in a ready-made manner, without considering the particular spiritual capacities of the receivers. One cannot avoid the impression that giving a hwadu to a student nowadays seems a little like mass production in a factory. Hwadus given in this fashion do not motivate the receivers to raise a real question, and in many cases the hwadu might not have any effect on their minds. So please tell us whether you could offer new hwadus that would be more suitable for people today, instead of the 1,700 old Seon dialogues and stories that are traditionally used, so that we could raise the deepest questioning more easily.

It is only your discriminative mind that causes you to blame the hwadu for your questioning being weak. What is most important is that you receive the hwadu with complete faith. You must diligently work on it regardless of whether the teacher gives you one of the 1,700 classic gongans, or gives you a word on the spot when you ask him a question. Authentic hwadu questioning never relies on what an enlightened master elucidates to you regarding this or that.

Of course, when a student comes and asks me a question either about the fundamental meaning of the buddhaDharma or "Why did Bodhidharma come from the West?" I'll give them an answer, just as the ancient masters used to do. Then you can turn it into homework to study. But these days there are very few people who really want to work with this sort of attitude. Everyone says, "I have come to you to receive a hwadu," so there's nothing I can do except take a chance and give them a hwadu of my choosing. Therefore, when working on a hwadu, the issue is not which hwadu the teacher gave you; instead, it is how sincerely you accept it and how seriously you work on it.

31. Is it all right to meditate with our eyes closed?

It might be all right to meditate with your eyes closed, if you can maintain your single-minded attention on the hwadu. But in nine cases out of ten, you will instead fall into delusion and sleepiness.

32. What about the various methods for controlling the breath?

I don't recommend any of them. Natural breathing is the best. If you try some special technique, it might well make things more difficult for your practice. So don't worry about what kind of breathing you do; just focus on your hwadu.

33. You told us to place the hwadu directly in front of our eyes. But if the hwadu is in front and the person who holds the hwadu is behind, doesn't this create a bifurcation between the meditative object and the meditating subject?

I mean only that all of your attention must be placed directly in front of your eyes. If you get familiar with placing the hwadu in front, you will be able to practice with ease whether sitting, walking, lying down, or eating: you will never be without your hwadu. If you hold the hwadu in your head, it may cause your qi-energy to rise and make you flushed. It would then be difficult to focus on the hwadu because you would be disturbed by what you see and hear.

34. Are you saying that we should "observe" the hwadu?

No, observing is the wrong expression. Hwadu is not an object to watch over quietly, but something that should engender profound questioning. Genuine questioning suddenly creates absorption in the single-mindedness of no-mind samadhi; then, oneself and the outside world vanish and "I" become just a mass of questioning. This mass of questioning is then free from both subject and object.

35. If we want this mass of questioning to continue unimpeded, don't we need to make an intentional effort to maintain it?

No, you don't need to make effort; it continues on its own.

36. If the single-mindedness of hwadu questioning is interrupted from time to time, does this mean we won't be able to sustain the practice?

It is a strict rule that this single-mindedness should continue without interruption. However, there is no set limit on how long it should continue—it could be days, months, or years; it differs from person to person. As for this mountain monk, it didn't take me so long.

DROPPING THE ANXIOUS MIND

37. What is the biggest reason that many practitioners do not achieve enlightenment, even though they might spend a lifetime at it?

First, those who do not succeed often have not had sufficient faith in an enlightened master. Second, they may not have received correct guidance. Anyone who wishes to reach this supreme goal should cut off all entanglements and make a firm determination to attain enlightenment.

38. Is it good for us to be examined whenever we encounter new stages in our practice?

Since the master's role is to listen to us and give right guidance, it is best to ask.

39. Which fault is bigger, to ask or not to ask?

When you want to go to Seoul, you need to go straight in the right direction, and not allow yourself to be led astray. Therefore you should take instruction from an enlightened master and go straight to Seoul without wasting any time.

40. Does age matter in attaining enlightenment?

Practice is not dependent on age, but only on how willing you are to accept guidance and hold on to the hwadu.

41. I'd like to ask about the matter of physical health. How did you manage your health before you were enlightened, how do you take care of yourself now, and are you still holding on to the hwadu now as your physical condition changes?

This body inevitably falls ill, whether it is healthy or not. Everybody has a little bit of sickness all the time, so we should not allow ourselves to become attached to this body. Your body may have a stomachache, or neuralgia, or a cold, and these things always come and go. But if you hold on to your hwadu and stay with it, your stomach disorder or neuralgia can be healed. If you think, "Oh! I am so weak, or I have some disease," and are so attached to this fear that you hesitate to practice, then you will never find a way out. Therefore, if you hold on to the hwadu without thinking of weak health or minor illnesses, those things will disappear naturally if you will just stay in this single-minded practice. Your mind will be detached from its obsession with illness and, naturally, your health will improve.

Moreover, when you maintain your upright posture in sitting meditation, all physical and mental obstacles will simply disappear. Your delusions and sleepiness will vanish. Therefore, the sitting posture is very important. If you habituate yourself to a correct posture, you can practice comfortably for a whole lifetime. You will be able to sit for a long time, and you won't feel a need to switch your legs up and down when they become painful.

As for diet, never eat just rich, delicious food, but eat a well-balanced diet and, most important, do not overeat.

An enlightened master accommodates the realized state in everyday life, even though he has completed his study. This means that the treasure of enlightenment is being used in all his daily activities.

42. How many hours a night do we have to sleep?

For people engaged in Seon practice, four or five hours of sleep a night is enough.

43. What do you think about sitting all night long without lying down to sleep?

I don't recommend these difficult ascetic practices. If you could sit all night long and not fall prey to drowsiness and fatigue, it would be all right, but forcing yourself to do so will just create trouble for your practice. If you hold on to your hwadu single-mindedly, you will be able to sit all day long naturally, and sleepiness and pain will vanish. But merely imitating what you have heard about monks doing, or following what you have read in books about the enlightenment experiences of certain ancient masters—this may harm your body and is of no use to the real work of enlightenment. Your body is like a machine that needs oil, so you should sleep at night and train yourself without sleepiness and delusion.

44. What do you think of eating just once a day, before noon, as the Buddha and his disciples did?

The time you eat is not the issue; you should always eat moderately in order to maintain your health.

45. Do you mean that if we hold on to the hwadu correctly, then such ascetic practices as day-long sittings, keeping strict silence, and eating just one meal a day will develop naturally, without having to force things?

That's right. You only need to hold on to your hwadu. That is all.

APPENDICES

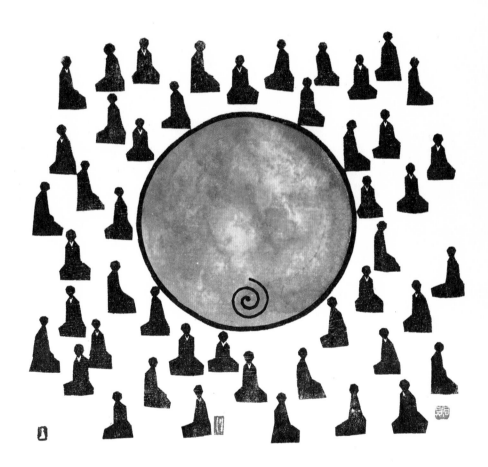

The Whole World is a Single Family:
the Human Race is a Single Body

A Dialogue between Master Jinje and Theologian Paul Knitter

Paul Knitter is the Paul Tillich Professor Emeritus of Theology, World Religions, and Culture at Union Theological Seminary in the New York City. A leading specialist in religious pluralism and interreligious dialogue, Professor Knitter is the author of many books, including Without Buddha I Could Not Be a Christian: A Personal Journey of Passing Over and Passing Back *(Oneworld Publications, 2009). Professor Knitter is especially known for bringing different religious communities together to collaborate on promoting human and ecological well-being.*

Professor Knitter visited South Korea in December, 2010, at the invitation of Master Jinje, in order to help foster reconciliation and dialogue between religions in Korea. During his visit on, Professor Knitter visited Master Jinje on New Year's Eve at his monastery of Donghwa-sa, outside the city of Daegu. The following is an edited transcript of the discussion that followed.

Master Jinje: Since this room is blocked by a high mountain, all the buddhas and awakened ones cannot see me. Professor Knitter, how are you going to see me?

Prof. Knitter: How do I see you? Well, I see you as a representative and embodiment of a deep spiritual tradition that is even older than my own tradition of Christianity. And it is a tradition from which I know that many Christians, myself included, have learned much—the Buddhist tradition in general, but especially the teachings of Zen and Seon. And I see this as a great opportunity. In today's world, it is crucial that religions work together and learn from each other.

Master Jinje: Oh, Prof. Knitter, you are indeed blessed! A long thread of the Buddha's mind seal is in Korea, and a strand of that thread continues right here, in Donghwa Temple, on Palgong Mountain. This monastery preserves the favorable conditions where the supreme Dharma can be heard and practiced. Also, Donghwa Temple has a 1600-year-old history. It is a sacred place, where some 1450 relics of Shakyamuni Buddha are preserved and venerated.

Many Seon monks of resolute spirit are gathered here: there are thirty monks meditating in the Geumdang Seon Meditation Hall, and another 150 Seon practitioners from all walks of life meditating in the main temple. They sit in intensive meditation for fourteen hours every day. Inspired monks from all around Korea totally devote themselves in this way, and they spend all their energy—some without sleeping—in order to inherit the Buddha's mind seal, which I myself hold. I deeply appreciate your visit to such a wonderful and sacred place of living practice.

Prof. Knitter: It is my honor. Sunim, one of the things that impressed me most as soon as I walked into this room was your serene and welcoming smile, the smile of enlightenment itself. I would certainly like to live the kind of contemplative life you describe going on here. If I practice as you have suggested and if I should come to an awakening about my true self, may I come back to check it with you?

Master Jinje: Of course, I will welcome you with open arms. Since you have taken such a rare step as this visit, I would like to ask you to continue to soak up Korean spiritual culture to the fullest, and please spread it to the entire world!

Prof. Knitter: Oh, we want very much to do that. But we will need some help.

Master Jinje: I will help you in any way I can.

Master Jinje and Professor Knitter then rose from their seats and walked out to the Main Buddha Hall, where a conference was being held on issues of Buddhist-Christian dialogue. There had been a heavy snowfall for several days; the temple precincts were thickly covered in white and the mountain peaks surrounding the temple were swathed in a gleaming white blanket. As the two of them passed under the ancient Bongseo pavilion, they both noticed three snowmen that visitors to the temple had made. Professor Knitter questioned Master Jinje.

Prof. Knitter: Sunim, are these snowmen enlightened?

Master Jinje: They were even before time immemorial. Ha!

Once inside the Main Buddha Hall, they took their seats, and the conversation continued.

Master Jinje: As you well know, Professor Knitter, we in Korea are in constant confrontation between North and South. In addition, the South Korean people are troubled by interreligious conflict. You, as a Christian, have come from far away, bringing your great concern about the religious situation in Korea. I truly thank you for your efforts. Just as you are doing, all Buddhists and Christians should work together to resolve conflicts and bring peace and happiness in the world. To guide people in the right way and to strive for world peace is the responsibility and mission of us all, but especially of religious leaders.

Prof. Knitter: Well, I can speak for the many Christians who are committed to working for peace, but we always say we must work for peace together with justice. Justice must go with peace. They need each other. What many are starting to realize—and what my wife Cathy and I realized during our work in the country of El Salvador during their civil war of the 1980s—is that we must have peace in our hearts before we can have peace in the world. That is a lesson we have learned especially well from our Buddhist brothers and sisters. We are realizing that we must be active in our pursuit of peace, we must work at it, but we also must stop to pray, to be silent, to take care of our own spirituality. So action and contemplation, or action and meditation, must operate together.

I would like to ask you a question about what I understand to be a pluralistic dimension of all religions. My question is this: We Christians believe that God can make God's truth known in many different ways.

We Christians use the word "salvation": to be saved. It is similar to the Buddhist word "enlightenment." These terms seem to me to be so much alike! Now, we believe that God can save people through many different religions. In the same way, do you believe that enlightenment is possible in many religions, not just in Buddhism?

Master Jinje: All religions exist for a reason, and that reason is to save the human race. Religions should guide people up the mountain of truth. Every religion has its own characteristics, but they vary in their depths. In this troubled world, every religious leader should focus his energy simply on guiding people to the land of peace and bliss, regardless of the perceived differences in their various teachings and practices.

The Buddha teaches us that universal truth is found in our true self. Everyone is equally endowed with the true self. The problem is simply that people remain ignorant of their true selves, and do not harness that reality in their everyday lives.

Hence, I wish to propagate Seon practice around the world, to awaken people to the true self that exists in their minds right now. This path is at the heart of Asian culture. Anyone who attains their true self comes to understand that it has neither beginning nor end. The arising and passing away of everything in the universe occurs on the ground of that true self.

Prof. Knitter: We Christians say something similar. We teach that the truth of who we really are is within ourselves; we speak about the Holy Spirit being present within us. And perhaps in the same way as you say that you are trying to realize your buddhanature, many Christians would say that we are trying to realize our Christ-nature, which is eternally within us.

But I might need some help in order to attain this realization. I would need someone to teach me, to guide me. I need a teacher. Of course, I find a teacher in Jesus, and I find a teacher in the Buddha. But sometimes we also may need help from "outside" to realize what we are "inside."

Master Jinje: The Buddha became enlightened to his true self. So the practice of Ganhwa Seon, or questioning meditation, which enables people today to realize their true selves, is really nothing other than the essence of the Buddha's enlightenment. According to legend, right after Siddhartha

Gautama realized his true self, he exclaimed, "In the heavens above and the earth below, I alone am venerated." This is how he demonstrated to the world that the true self is in itself already complete and endowed with wisdom and equality. For this reason, I encourage you to take up the deep interior questioning of Ganhwa Seon so that you, too, may attain the same wisdom and equality as the Buddha himself.

Prof. Knitter: So, Sunim, we have spoken about what Christians need to learn from Buddhist practitioners like yourself. Clearly, one of the most important things that we Christians can learn from Buddhism is how to work within oneself in meditation. Now, with all due respect, in the spirit of this dialogue, I would like to ask if perhaps there is something that Buddhists might learn from Christians?

We Christians are beginning to realize that we need to learn from Buddhists how to be at peace, how to discover our true self through practice. But Christians also believe that it is important—it is an essential part of being "saved" or "enlightened," in fact—to act in the world and in society, to get involved in the world. We believe that it is urgent to change this world in which there is so much suffering—suffering because of social injustice, unfair economic policies, or certain political policies. This need to engage in social and political action is a part of the work of enlightenment, is it not? Would you agree with such a claim?

Master Jinje: All Buddhists certainly admire the Protestant and Catholic practice of serving and loving your fellow man. But Buddhists take self-perfection as the primary matter. When you realize self-perfection, you will automatically act as a Buddha or an enlightened being. You can lead people to a land of peace and comfort. When you are not doing the inner work of becoming awakened fully to your true self, however, you are not really able to guide people.

For this reason, as a Seon monk, I strive to guide people to find their true self by means of deep interior questioning. When you go up the hill of truth, you will be endowed with the 84,000 Dharma teachings. The sole mission of an enlightened master is to deliver everyone to the other shore of wisdom and nirvana. Only then will you attain the point the Buddha made when he said, "In the heavens above and the earth below, I alone am venerated." This insight was not something gained from a book or a tradition. The Buddha attained this view through arduous self-perfection, from his own meditation practice that looked deeply into the inner world of his mind. One taste of Korean Seon practice is enough to enable you to understand what he meant by saying, "I alone am venerated."

Prof. Knitter: I believe you. I know that what you say is true. But help me because I have a problem in one regard—you said that one must first realize one's true self before one goes out to act in the world for the benefit of others. You emphasize that I have to achieve nirvana in order to do this work of helping, saving, liberating. And yet, while I am sitting, doing my meditation, children are starving and people are being tortured. There is incredible racial injustice in so many parts of the world. And so, as I sit, trying to discover my true self, I cannot help but hear the cries of these suffering people. Do I really have to master this practice first before I can act? How long do I have to wait for there to be some fruit?

Master Jinje: The Buddhist teachings include the two aspects of Samantabhadra's "activity" and Manjusri's "wisdom." There is the fully altruistic way of practice, as inspired by Samantabhadra, where one first enacts one's aspiration to deliver all beings into liberation before going on to attain one's own enlightenment. This is a very important strain of Buddhist belief. On the other hand, there is the equally valid path of holding off on such altruistic activities, and exerting oneself instead to become completely endowed with the correct eye of truth, as inspired by Manjusri's wisdom. Such an attainment would not just be "private," or "personal"; it would qualify one to engage in spiritual leadership, to guide people to liberation. So, in Buddhism, these two paths exist side by side and do not exclude each other.

Prof. Knitter: So it would be correct, then, to state that we have to practice, but, at the same time, we have to act in the world; both tracks are necessary. Sunim, is it correct, then, to characterize your view as saying that although we have both to engage others and to practice, practice is more important?

Master Jinje: In the Buddhist tradition, endowing oneself with the correct eye of truth comes first. One must strive to have clear eyes first, for only then can you guide people to any kind of real liberation. If you are blind, how can you guide people to a land of peace? In that sense, we teach practitioners to "see their true natures." Since the true self is the whole point of this teaching, seeing directly into your true self enables you to see directly into the state of this suffering world.

In Korea, most large monasteries have established Seon meditation halls, where intrepid practitioners work hard, through intensive meditation, to awaken their correct Dharma eye. Only in this way can we lead people to a land of bliss.

Now, spiritual seekers in every Seon meditation hall throughout Korea focus their efforts on "see your true nature and become a buddha." In order for them to engage in this long and lonely practice, many supporting personnel—such as abbots and temple directors—are constantly engaged in altruistic activities that support the community of meditating monks. Thus, in Korea, the two wheels of wisdom and action run very well together.

If you look at history, you will see that Buddhists never created conflicts or initiated wars for the sake of their religious beliefs. This fact alone should be proof enough that when people engage in meditation, and through their own efforts reach the home of their mind-nature, the earth becomes a single family. The material and the immaterial are revealed to be nondual and at one with you and me. Since you and I are not two, how then could there be any strife and animosity?

Prof. Knitter: Thank you for this excellent teaching! I have two follow-up questions. One is a personal one for you, Sunim, and the other one is for me. The personal question is this: As a Christian, I would like to know a little more about your own path of practice. How did you, in your own life, come to practice the way you do? Please tell me how you came to the experience of enlightenment, so that perhaps I can learn from you, from your own path, and from your own personal experience.

Master Jinje: I joined the Buddhist monastic order when I was twenty years old. After I wrestled with the deep interior questioning on the hwadu for some three or four years, all of sudden I thought that I had reached the truth. I went to see the great Seon Master Hyanggok, so he could examine whether my insight was complete or partial. In those days, Master Hyanggok was a great leader and teacher whose own spiritual insights had been sanctioned and who had thus inherited the main lineage of Korean Seon. Entering his room, I prostrated to him three times, and said, "I've come to have my view examined."

Without even a perfunctory greeting, Master Hyanggok shouted, "If you speak, I will hit you thirty times with my staff; if you stay silent, I will hit you thirty times with my staff! What do you do?"

I was at a total loss for words! He thundered back, "So you can't even answer this one simple question! How dare you come here, thinking you know something!"

He then questioned me about a famous story, well known in Seon circles: the story of Nanquan's cat.

A long time ago in China, some seven hundred monks practiced Seon meditation in the temple of Seon Master Nanquan. The monastery had a cat that was cared for by the monks of both residential wings of the monastery. The monks of the eastern hall claimed the cat as their favorite pet, while the monks of the western hall claimed the cat as theirs. There were sometime disagreements over the proper care and feeding of the temple cat. So, one day, a huge dispute broke out in the temple.

Learning of this dispute, Master Nanquan ordered his attendant to strike the temple bell, calling all of the temple residents together. All seven hundred monks dropped what they were doing and gathered in the main Dharma Hall. The master ascended the Dharma seat and ordered his attendant: "Bring me the cat and a knife."

Lifting the cat with one hand, and holding the knife with the other, Nanquan exclaimed to the assembly, "All you Seon practitioners have been arguing over a cat. You both claim this cat as your own. Monks of the eastern and western halls, give me one word to save this cat. If you cannot, I will cut the cat in half!"

Seeing this, a great hue and cry went up from the assembly.

Some monks shouted, "It's our cat!" Other monks shouted, "It's our cat!" All of them remained stuck in their petty dispute. Since none of them could give a satisfactory answer, Master Nanquan sliced the cat in two and returned to his room.

Some hours later, Nanquan's most accomplished student, Zhaozhou, returned to the temple after finishing some business in the market. Master Nanquan related to him the happenings of the day. "Today I taught the assembly of monks about this cat," Master Nanquan said. "If you had been there, what would you have done to save it?"

Hearing this, Zhaozhou immediately placed his pair of grass sandals on top of his head and left the room. Nanquan sighed and said, "Ah, Zhaozhou, if only you had been in the assembly we could have saved that cat."

This seemingly inscrutable action on Zhaozhou's part suggests that simply placing a pair of grass sandals on one's head might be an appropriate solution for this difficult question of life and death. So, Master Hyanggok asked me, "Tell me why Zhaozhou placed a pair of grass sandals on his head and went away?"

I was at a total loss for words. Master Hyanggok threw me out of his room, saying: "You stupid monk! How come you trumpet forth about realizing something when you can't even understand this question?"

From that day on, I practiced Seon meditation for two years at various Seon halls. I strove diligently to prepare my mind to meet a clear-eyed master so that my practice would continue in the right direction. Wandering here and there like clouds and water, I lived out of my monk's backpack from retreat season to retreat season.

One day, when I was 26 years old, I went to see Master Hyanggok again. I entreated him, "Master, give me a hwadu."

"How can you get through this great barrier, which is so difficult and demanding?" he shot back.

I promised him, "I will devote my whole body and mind to this practice."

Sensing the sincerity of my statement, Master Hyanggok gave me a hwadu. Bowing in eternal gratitude for his intervention and assistance in my study of the self, I said, "I will not pick up my backpack again to travel until I have broken through this hwadu."

I grappled with this hwadu for about two years and five months, struggling with all my heart. Every single day during that period, I woke up at 3 a.m., rolled up my bedding, and went straight to the Buddha Hall for the morning service. It was always dark outside at that time of night and the monastery had no exterior lighting. One morning, on the way to services, I tripped over a paving stone. The moment I got up, the hwadu completely shattered.

In those days, the hwadu that I was using was the case of Xiangyan climbing a tree. Here is the story behind this hwadu:

> Someone is dangling by his mouth from a tall tree. His hands are tied behind his back and there's nothing beneath his feet. Someone appears under the tree and asks him, "What is the meaning of Bodhidharma's coming from the West?"
> If you keep your mouth clenched and refuse to answer, you will forsake the questioner. If you open your mouth to answer, you will fall to your death. What do you do?"

After tripping over that paving stone, I had broken through the barrier of the hwadu. I composed a verse of enlightenment and presented it to Master Hyanggok:

> How many people have known this Seon staff?
> None of the sages of past, present, or future recognize it.
> This Seon staff transforms into a golden dragon
> Whose responses are limitless and occur entirely at will.

Master Hyanggok read the poem; he did not comment on the first two lines at all. But taking up the next two lines, he threw a question at me like a thunderbolt: "When the dragon meets a garuda, what will you do?"

In Asian culture, a garuda is a mythical bird that beats the sea with its wings when it's hungry, splitting sea water ten miles away; it then dives into the deep sea and snatches the dragons that are under the sea to eat. Master Hyanggok was asking me how I would react if I came across this fearsome bird.

So I responded, "I will bend my body at the chest, and move backward three steps."

Suddenly, Master Hyanggok roared back, "Ah, right you are! Correct!"

Having solved this gongan case, I was free to give Dharma talks and teach. Nothing hindered me in practice or teaching. And yet there was still one gongan I could not break through:

> Master Mazu was close to death. His attendant monk asked after the venerable master's health every morning: "Master, did you sleep well last night?" Mazu would answer, "Sun-faced Buddha, moon-faced Buddha."

After relating this story to me one day, Master Hyanggok asked, "What did Master Mazu mean when he said 'Sun-faced Buddha, moon-faced Buddha'?"

I was at a total loss for words. For some five years, I devoted all my energy to questioning this hwadu.

I had spent nine years practicing Seon meditation at Myogwaneum Temple. Because that monastery is located in the extreme southern part of the Korean peninsula, it seldom snows. But one morning, during the first month of the year according to the lunar calendar, I saw snow blanketing the hills and the seashore surrounding the temple. While walking around a corner of a building, I saw a big bucket filled utterly to the brim with water. No snow had accumulated in the bucket because snowflakes melt in water. At that very instant the hwadu shattered.

I broke through this tough hwadu only after a five-year-long effort. I then composed another enlightenment verse and presented it directly to Master Hyanggok:

> One strike of this staff knocks Vairocana over his head;
> One thunderous shout wipes away ten million cases.
> In this small thatched hut, I stretch out my legs.
> A fresh breeze over the ocean is eternally renewed.

Reading this poem, Master Hyanggok praised me, saying, "The deepest meanings of the Sixth Patriarch, Master Mazu, and even Linji's family tradition sing out from these lines!"

In the year of the Fire Goat (1967), Master Hyanggok ascended the high Dharma seat and prepared to give a Dharma talk in the Main Buddha Hall of Myogwaneum Temple. It was the closing ceremony for the ninety-day summer intensive retreat. I rose before the assembly, prostrated three times, and said: "Master, I do not want to ask about something the Buddha and patriarchs know. Would you please tell me instead what the Buddha and patriarchs don't know?"

Master Hyanggok replied, "Nine times nine is eighty-one."

"That is what the Buddha and patriarchs know."

"Six times six is thirty-six."

Upon hearing this, I bowed and departed, without saying whether it was right or wrong. Master Hyanggok continued, "I have completed today's Dharma talk," and promptly descended from the high Dharma seat.

The next day, putting on formal robes, I went to the master's room and asked again, "I do not ask about the Buddha eye or the correct Dharma eye. But what is the correct Dharma eye of this patch-robed monk?"

Master Hyanggok replied, "An old Buddhist nun congenitally performs woman's work."

"Today, I saw you in person for the first time," I replied. "For the last nine years, we stayed together and got along in every action. But today, I peeped into your enlightened secret. Ah-ha—so this is what it means!"

Master Hyanggok asked back, "And where did you see me?"

I shouted, "*Gwan!*"

With this answer, he sanctioned my endowment of an eye of truth and bestowed on me the certificate of authorization he had inherited from the Buddha:

> *Bestowed to Patriarch Jinje Boepwon:*
> The great live word of the buddhas and patriarchs
> Can be neither transmitted nor received.
> Today I entrust this live word to you,
> Whether you hold it or release it is entirely up to you.

This is the way of transmission in Korean Ganhwa Seon; this is how the essence of Korean Seon is expressed and confirmed. It is a tradition descended from the Buddha until now.

Prof. Knitter: Well, that kind of prepares me for my second question, which concerns the Dharma name you gave me this morning. My Dharma name is "True Self" (Jin-a), which also serves as my hwadu. I must say that I was very moved when you gave me this name. The notion of true self is also found in the Christian scriptures, in the Bible. We are asked to realize and discover our true selves. But it is also one of the things that I feel, as a Christian, we can learn from your tradition.

Is hwadu the same as koan practice? You told me that I should keep this question, "What was I before my parents conceived me?" You told me I should keep a ball of doubt and keep asking the question: "Who am I?" "What is my true self?"

So you are telling me just to keep practicing, to keep this question in mind when I am walking, when I am sleeping, and when I am talking—not to lose contact with it during any activity. But should I just wait for enlightenment, then? My question is this (and this may be a typically Christian question): Can I be sure that there will finally be that moment when enlightenment occurs? Can I trust that this will happen before I die?

Master Jinje: The practice of seeing into your true nature and realizing enlightenment is possible anytime and anywhere. You should simply raise the question, "What is my true self from before I was born?" Just continue this questioning, day and night, with total devotion and purposefulness, like the mind of a parent yearning to see again his long-lost only son. Then, if you practice in this way, you won't be bothered by what you see and what you hear; you won't have any sense of time passing or of where you are. Anyone, regardless of gender or age, can reach this level. The key to awakening is how long and steady the single-mindedness of the hwadu questioning continues. If the earnest questioning continues on without interruption, you might think that just a moment has passed, but in fact days or months may have already elapsed. When you arrive at this state, you may unexpectedly see or hear something that causes the hwadu to shatter. In that instant, you will have reached the status of a Buddha right where you are standing, without moving a single step. This process can be completed only under the guidance of a clear-eyed enlightened master. You cannot succeed on your own.

Prof. Knitter: So, the Buddha emphasizes the need to realize your true self and then to act. And Jesus is talking about the need to involve yourself for the sake of justice, for the sake of stopping the sufferings of others caused by oppressive political structures. Both approaches are necessary, and I think they both can speak to each other.

Master Jinje: Religions should all aim to guide people to a land of peace and bliss, shouldn't they? Each religion has its own virtue. In the future, all religious leaders should strive to find common ground in order to save the world.

Eyes of the World On Supreme Patriarch Jinje & Korean Buddhism

The following is from a March 29, 2013, interview with Rabbi Jack Bemporad on BTN (Korean Buddhist TV), following Master Jinje's installation as Supreme Patriarch of the Jogye Order.

Rabbi Jack Bemporad currently serves as Professor of Interreligious Studies at the Vatican's Angelicum University in Rome and is the author of numerous books and articles, including Our Age: The Historic New Era of Christian-Jewish Understanding.

BTN: Hello. Thank for coming today. What was your experience of the Supreme Patriarch ceremony?

Rabbi Bemporad: What Master Jinje said in his Dharma talk was, to my mind, very important. He wanted to show that meditation is not simply a private matter of self-realization; he wanted to show that through this process a person can overcome one's self-centeredness and see his connection to all other human beings. I was very impressed with the latter part of his Dharma talk in which he said, "I am one with everyone and everyone is one with me—we are all interconnected." It reminded me of that marvelous passage from the prophet Isaiah, in chapter 58: "Don't separate yourself from your own flesh." The other person is your flesh.

But how can you get to that stage? How can you come to that realization that you are not a separate entity, self centered, egotistical, only concerned about yourself, but really transcend all that and gain a perspective that will enable you to encompass all human beings, all of creation?

BTN: How did you meet Master Jinje?

Rabbi Bemporad: My main work for the last thirty years has been to have the top leadership of all religions communicate and have genuine dialogue with one another. For example, I've had eight audiences with Pope John Paul the II and three audiences with Pope Benedict III. I work with Muslim leaders all over the world; I felt it was very important to have authentic Buddhist representation as part of the whole interreligious dialogue. When I heard Master Jinje was coming to United States, I arranged to have him meet the top leadership in the Jewish, Christian, and Muslim worlds.

It so happened we were having a meeting in Long Island and so I was able to arrange for him to come speak to some of the top religious leaders in the United States. When I brought Master Jinje to meet with them, he just said a few words about his background, his particular way of meditating, and so forth. Then he opened himself up to questions. The people who were there were so amazed at his authenticity.

That led to my organizing his visit to Washington, D.C. at the National Prayer Breakfast with representatives from Congress, the Senate, and the diplomatic community of the world. I also invited the top religious leadership in New York City to meet with Master Jinje and my center, the Center for Interreligious Understanding, sponsored a lunch in his honor. We had the top religious leadership of New York City come, and here again, what was interesting was that he spoke and there were very, very tough questions. They were not used to Buddhists, but he got a standing ovation. They were so impressed with his responses.

BTN: What was your first impression of Master Jinje?

Rabbi Bemporad: His very presence, the way he carried himself, his tremendous modesty, his willingness to accept questions, and his eagerness to help others—there was nothing self-centered about him. He is genuinely with you. And people respond to that.

BTN: As a world religious figure yourself, how do you think about Master Jinje as a religious leader?

Rabbi Bemporad: I think that what we have here is a truly enlightened teacher who has great things to teach; he should get a hearing. Now the question is, how do you get a Korean leader who speaks Korean and who, until recently, has been limited to Korea—how do you get this person a hearing in the world? That is the question that I am asking myself. And that's the question that I'm going to try to answer so that hopefully he will have a more important role among world religious leaders than he's had in the past. I see this is as a special obligation that I would like to take up.

BTN: In your opinion, what work should religious leaders be doing, and what do you expect from Master Jinje?

Rabbi Bemporad: I think that religious leadership today should recognize that we live in an interreligious world. We no longer live on isolated islands where we're just concerned about ourselves, not concerned about others. Religions have tremendous power because they speak for millions of people. And the question is, how can they use that power for good? How can they use that power to create peace and harmony among religions rather than conflict and hatred? That's the task. In the past, all too often, religions have treated other religions in terrible ways.

Let me give you a very good example of progress. Imam Ibrahim Sayar, who represents the Muslim leaders in the United States, recently said something very interesting. He said "In the past, it was only Judaism, Christianity, and Islam—all other religions were ignored." But then he added, "We now come to the realization that we have to dialogue with Buddhism." It's an incredible, incredible revolution in the Muslim world to have a Muslim leader say that dialogue with the Buddhist community is a central element of interreligious dialogue. In the past, that was impossible for them. Now, why can't we use this window of opportunity, where you have religious leaders who are willing to talk to one another, who are willing to assemble together? Why not do it? With this in mind, I feel a certain obligation to work to make Master Jinje a representative all over the world on behalf of Buddhism.

BTN: Do you have anything else you would like to say about Master Jinje?

Rabbi Bemporad: All I can say is that the ceremony we saw yesterday was the elevation of a superb, magnificent, wonderful human being who has all of the requisites for genuine, authentic leadership. I just hope the audience recognizes this and gives him their total support.

About the Monk Jinje Beopwon

Jinje Beopwon was born in 1934 in Namhae, on the southern edge of the Republic of South Korea. He entered monastic life following an encounter at the age of 20 with Seon Master Seoku, at that time one of the most revered teachers in Korea. Fully ordained at 22 years old, he soon took up training under the guidance of the esteemed teacher Seon Master Hyanggok, who initiated Jinje into hwadu, the practice of investigating a single question for months or years to the exclusion of all other mental inquiry. This single-minded pursuit of realization culminated in 1967, when Jinje burst through his hwadu and received Dharma transmission from Master Hyanggok, a recognition of Jinje's standing in Korea as the 79th Patriarch in the lineage stretching back to Shakyamuni Buddha. Four years later, in 1971, he founded the monastery of Haeunjeong-sa, located in Busan. Since 2012 he has served as head of the Jogye Order, the largest Buddhist order in Korea, with the title of "Supreme Patriarch," guiding tens of thousands of monks and millions of laypeople on the path to enlightenment. Jinje's work is an expression of his commitment to spread Dharma through Seon practice and to collaborate with religious leaders for world peace.